"Casanova Fly & the Disco Wiz, that was us. After our lives were divided by circumstance, I stuck fast to the Hip Hop route I was sure would eventually bring me fame and glory, as we used to say. I went through many different line-ups after finally settling in with The Cold Crush Brothers. I had reached that status that Wiz and I sought and fought for, but without my original partner. I'd like to think I've carried a part of him with me throughout my journey. This book should shed some light on Wiz as a person, father, husband, friend, cancer survivor, and pioneer of Hip Hop."

— Grandmaster Caz

"*It's Just Begun* took me back to when I first came from Cuba in 1971, and most importantly it took me back to the very essence of what I would become later in life."

— Mellow Man Ace

"Even as a genuine pioneer of an art form now spanning the longer part of 40 years, Disco Wiz has remained humble in his dedication to Hip Hop culture. No matter the accolades, no matter the recognition, no matter the stature, Wiz is a living reminder that perseverance, diligence, and hard work do eventually pay off. It's been a long time coming, but DJ Disco Wiz can now take his rightful place in history."

— Carlito Rodriguez, Former Editor-In-Chief,
The Source Magazine

"Riveting and truthful — its haunting words leave you speechless. A cautionary tale for some, a confessionary truth for others, *It's Just Begun* will have you pinned to your seat throughout the night. You'll be reading it with your nightlight on, a box of tissues at your side, and your heart in your throat."

— Jeff Rivera, *Forever My Lady*

"*It's Just Begun* is a gritty and emotional express ride through the South Bronx of yesterday and the life and times of one of Hip Hop's unsung heroes - DJ Disco Wiz. Urban non-fiction at its absolute best!"

— James "Koe" Rodriguez

IT'S JUST BEGUN

IT'S ☆ JUST ☆ BEGUN

THE EPIC JOURNEY OF DJ DISCO WIZ, HIP HOP'S FIRST LATINO DJ

BY IVAN SANCHEZ
AND LUIS "DJ DISCO WIZ" CEDEÑO

pH powerHouse Books Brooklyn, NY

Miss Rosen Editions

This book is dedicated to my Immortal beloved Lizette who nurtured me with unconditional love and believed in me when I no longer believed in myself.
—Luis "DJ Disco Wiz" Cedeño

"Our biggest fear is not that we are inadequate. Our deepest fear is that we are powerful beyond measure."
—Marianne Williamson

This book is dedicated to those few two percent who help me soldier on with this mission called life. My familia for uplifting me when I no longer want to uplift myself. To Heaven, Starr & Anesa... Everything I do in this life is for you.
—*Ivan Sanchez*

"One should count each day a separate life."
—*Lucius Annaeus Seneca*

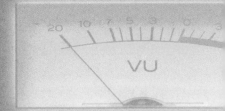

LEFT ———————————— RIGHT

MIC 2   MIC 2   MIC 3

PAN POT   PAN POT   PAN POT

L · R   L · R   L · R

L · R   L · R   L · R

Table of Contents

MONITOR LEVEL

REALISTIC

STEREO MIXING CONSOLE

POWER

PHONO - TAPE/AUX

MASTER VOLUME

CUE

CUE

MONO ⌐ STEREO

— IN
🔲 OUT

— IN
🔲 OUT

PHONO ⌐   ⌐ TAPE

PHONO ⌐   ⌐ AUX

10
9
8
7
6
5
4
3
2
1
0

track 07: Don't Know What… We're Running From

track 08: You Gotta Do Your Thing

track 09: Once We Have Togetherness

track 10: That's The Scene

track 11: We Had Fun

track 12: It's Just Begun

FADER

5 4 3 2 1 0 1 2 3 4 5

The Product

I am the prodigal son, and I was born on holy
*   ground, yes its true I come from mecca*
I am the product of many but I am no one and no one
*   is me, then again I am all that can ever be. You see*
*   these streets sang to me in sweet urban lullabies,*
I am the product of kings and queens Mayan Aztec taino dreams
That never die, I am that spicy version of your American apple pie.

I am a product of uprisings revolutionary movements and
*   my ancestors' cries*
But if you choose to swim in these waters, be ready to die,
*   cause you might have too.*
Some things in this life are just worth that much.

Track One: Watch Me Now... Fill the Room

For as far back as I can remember music has always been the backdrop and recurring theme of my life. It has been the seemly soothing remedy to my problems, and for many years at least, I could say that I was able to find joy in the sweet, melodic melody of music. It would feed my soul when I was hungry, make me laugh when I wanted to cry, and show me another side to life that would fulfill me in my emptiest of times. No song would feed my existence more profoundly than "It's Just Begun" by the Jimmy Castor Bunch. Although the song wouldn't be released for a full eleven years until after my birth, it might as well have been playing in the delivery room as my mother introduced me to the world. The lyrics became prophetic to the path I would walk upon this earth as well as the anthem of the Hip Hop movement.

There could be no words more symbolic of how many times our lives had to start over. Each day brought new challenges in the Boogie Down Bronx and each day allowed us the opportunity to awaken to a fresh start in our search for sanity. The Bronx in the 1960s and 70s resembled the remains of a war zone, with miles of abandoned buildings and empty lots. From my window, I had the perfect view of a policy of "benign neglect," as the politicians treated the Bronx and the people in it as disposable. Their allies, the slumlords, burned down buildings, collected the insurance money, and relocated to the suburbs to rebuild, reinvest, and raise their own families in a much different surrounding.

As a result of the economic and environmental destitution, the community changed as radically as the landscape. Small time hoods trying to feed their families were running numbers rackets, selling dope, and committing robberies. Gangs were running in packs, whether for protection or intimidation. The lawlessness led to a lot of violent and senseless crime in the city. This is the place into which I was born, on August 11, 1961.

Thirty-three years earlier, my mother, Anna Cira Garcia was born in Pinal Del Rio, Cuba, in 1928. She was the baby sister in a family with four brothers. Both of her parents died when she was very young so her older brother Candido raised her until 1958, when Fidel Castro came into power. While Fidel had promised to hand Cuba back over to the countrymen, peasants, and farmers, my mother had very bad feelings about Castro's takeover because her family lost their farmland and were forced to move out of their home. Sold on tales of gold-lined streets in America, my mother followed her brothers and other family members to Miami before choosing to venture out on her own. In 1959, she arrived in New York City completely alone.

I've often thought of my mother as being just as tough as the men who marched with Che Guevara in the revolutionary 26th of July Movement. Men who continued marching and fighting for the people of Cuba even after they had contracted mazamorra, a foot disease that made each and every step the soldiers took intolerable. My mother would have to take many of the same intolerable steps to keep her family moving in the right direction, and without that Cuban heart, the heart of those soldiers, I'm not sure she would have survived the struggles she faced in the trash-lined streets of New York. My mother didn't find gold when she arrived in the Bronx but she remained resilient.

Shortly after arriving in the United States my mother was introduced to my father, Alberto Nieves Cedeño, by her cousin Luis. They married within months. A year later, I was born in the Bronx and given the name Luis Alberto Cedeño.

My father was born in Toa Alta, Puerto Rico, in 1932. He had three brothers, Heño, Eddie, and Mario, as well as three sisters, Zaida, Carmen, and Sheffa. My grandmother Virginia was the head of the family, and she left Puerto Rico in the 1950s to get away from my abusive grandfather, Norberto. No one really spoke of my grandfather much as a person but always praised his artwork. Norberto Cedeño was born in 1897 in Tao Alta, PR, and he would go on to become famous for his sculpture, *La Mano Poderosa*, which translates in English to, *The All Powerful Hand of Christ*. In this work made of wood, St. Anne, her husband St. Joachim, their daughter the Virgin Mary, and her husband St. Joseph, are presented on each finger of the hand. The child Jesus lies on the thumb, as it is said that without the thumb the rest of the hand would be useless. Today this sculpture resides at El Museo del Barrio, on Fifth Avenue in New York City.

I don't know a great deal about my father's early history but I can recall hearing stories of how he helped the Coast Guard find the dead bodies of drowning victims in Bayamon, Puerto Rico, where he lived before moving to New York. If there is anything good I know of my father, it is that he loved the sea—and going fishing with my father and younger brother are some of my fondest memories as a child.

My brother Ricardo, who we call Rico, was born on September 30, 1962. My brother was always a good kid and a real homebody. He was very smart and hung out with a lot of geeks. We always got along as kids; he brought out the good in me. I was comfortable being myself with him, whether it was laughing at some really stupid shit, reading comics, building models, or our favorite pastime, watching scary movies, the TV series *Creature Features*, and *Chiller Theatre*—that was our shit.

When I was five years old we moved into 2350 Ryer Avenue in 1966 where *mi abuela* lived with her second husband, the building's superintendent. In addition to my grandmother, my aunts, my uncles, and my cousins all called the building home. Every day was a family reunion, which made it feel like it was *our* neighborhood. My favorite aunt was Zaida, she was like a big sister to me; I remember breaking nights in her apartment playing Monopoly. She was very cool and would try her best to keep me off the streets, even to the point of beating my ass in public. She was tough and always kept it real with me. I also looked up to *mi tío* Mario tremendously. If I wanted to be like any one man in my family at that time it unquestionably would have been him. Young, hip, and cool, Mario was a ladies man and everyone in the neighborhood admired him.

Kids were always in the streets, the alleyways, and rooftops, on the stoops, or in the lobbies of buildings playing neighborhood games that were passed down by the older generation, like skellzies whose roots can be traced back to the early 1900s. On the concrete floor we would draw a skelly board with chalk. The board was made up of numbered boxes and the object of the game was to make it from square one to the end of the board. We usually used bottle caps with melted wax as our weapon of choice. The heavier the shooter, the better chance you had of knocking the other kids off the board or of avoiding being knocked off the board yourself. We spent countless hours lying on hot concrete in the parks and sometimes right in

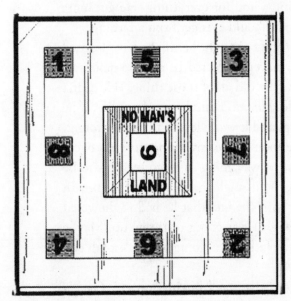

the middle of the street. We also spent hours playing ringolevio, stoop ball, and stickball and, my favorite, watching the girls in the neighborhood play double-dutch.

In the first grade I entered P.S. 9 Ryer Avenue Elementary School, but my public school career was over by the third grade. Like many Latinas, my mother believed, "If I give my children a Catholic school education, they will have a much better chance to succeed at life," so she enrolled me in Saint Simon Stock Catholic School. In Catholic school they had an interesting perspective on life: they preached a lesson of turn the other cheek. *Didn't they know that message just didn't fly in our neighborhoods?* There were times when I wanted to scream out to the priests and nuns, "Do you see what's going on outside the window!"

What my mother didn't realize was that growing up on the streets had as much to do—if not more—with our success as actual schooling. The neighborhood was my training ground and I learned the code of the streets on Ryer Avenue and the surrounding areas like Tiebout, Valentine, and Creston Avenues. It didn't take long for me to discover my fists were the best teachers of all.

As a child, I had a stuttering problem. Sometimes I would stutter when I got really excited about something or when I was stressed out, but I never did when I was relaxed, happy, or creative, be it drawing or painting, building models, or listening to music. Some of the kids on the block use to call me *Gago* (stutter) and I hated that fucking name more than anything in the world. Young kids don't really feel compassion towards others who are different, so whether you are the fat kid, the Latino or black kid, the poorest kid, or if you stutter, like I did, you are going to be put through hell and back. But I wasn't an easy target. Like my father, I chose violence to resolve conflict.

The neighborhood tough guy, my father came home many a night bruised up from his legendary street fights. He was passionate about drinking, and when he was drunk, he was extremely abusive. In hindsight, my father had a great deal of inadequacies and the only power he felt came from him putting his hands on people. Unfortunately, my mother, brother, and I were the people he spent the most time around and my father beat us for nothing, for anything, and for everything. He got more pleasure out of beating his family than any man should ever get from anything.

If my father would have remained sober long enough, he might have learned a thing or two from my mother. My father never protected us and he definitely didn't shelter us or feed us. It was my mother who did all of those things. He didn't do any of the things a father is supposed to do. He never taught me about life. If he did teach me anything, it was only one thing, and it was a lesson I'd rather forget.

When I was seven or eight years old he took me to my grandmother's backyard, the alley behind our building, and said he was going to teach me how to be a man. As he marched me down the stairs I could smell the alcohol on his breath and coming through his pores. Couple that with the fact that he hadn't showered in a few days and I remember feeling as though I was going to throw up. Maybe being a man meant being drunk, so maybe my father was going to drink a tall can of Budweiser with me.

Instead, he told me that he was going to "give me a boxing lesson." *Cool, a boxing lesson!* I put my hands up to emulate what I had seen on TV and what my father was now doing. *WHAP!!!* Damn that hurt. My father punched me right in the face. All I could see were stars. *WHAP!!!* He followed up with another punch. *This motherfucker was throwing combinations at his little boy.* I was a puny kid but I did the best I could not to let him see my fear or my pain—I didn't want to give him the satisfaction of seeing me cry. When he beat me I held it in and that made him more upset. He started hitting me harder and harder while taunting me with insults at the same time. He told me that I was going to cry before he was done beating me, but that never happened. I wished I were bigger so that I could fight back and knock him on his ass but all I managed to get in were a few shots I am sure he never felt.

Maybe my father felt if he taught me how to take a beat down from a man, I'd always be able to take whatever these mean streets of the Bronx would throw my way, but this is most likely just wishful thinking on my part. That day, my father damaged the little boy I was and the young man I would become. For years, I had trouble eating and became malnourished as a result. I was a very nervous child, never knowing when to expect the next beating or, even worse, when I had to sit idly by and watch him attack my mother.

My father didn't teach me how to be a man that day, he didn't teach me how to take a beating, he didn't teach me anything. The only thing my father accomplished that day was teaching me how to hate. The kind of hate that changes your perspective on life until you realize this hatred will cause your own self-destruction. The kind of hate I could never match and would never want to pass along to anyone in this world. Oh, my father taught me plenty in my lifetime, but not one of those lessons was positive.

★　★　★　★　★

BOOM, BOOM, BOOM, BOOM…
BOOM, BOOM, BOOM, BOOM…

The knocking at our front door was loud and loud knocking was never a good thing. I watched my father cautiously, but quickly, walk towards the door. A family relative burst in shouting, "MARIO IS DEAD!" and with those words I saw my father transform from angry drunk into grieving brother, crying and screaming at the same time, trying to get more information about how his younger brother had died. Just like that, I was introduced to not just death but to suicide for the first time.

A teenager in the neighborhood witnessed his death. Mario had asked him and a friend to walk with him into an alley. There, Mario asked the two teens to hold his jewelry and his wallet; they thought it was a little strange but quickly complied. Then Mario pulled a .45 caliber out of his waistband. As the kids turned to run away, they heard the gun go off. *Mi tío*, who was just thirty years old, had chosen to end his life in a dirty alley in the Bronx.

Apparently Mario had found out that his wife was cheating on him. As Puerto Rican men, we are very jealous, quick tempered, and passionate by nature and can be driven to madness when we feel slighted by a woman. Maybe Mario decided to kill himself rather than take the life of the mother of his two children, but his suicide was a decision I would never respect. The only ones left to suffer are the children. Shortly after his death, his wife would be shamed into moving out of the neighborhood; I never saw her or my cousins again. I still wonder how she lives with herself knowing her cheating ways caused the father of her children to take his own life.

I was only seven years old but I realized that death was final, and no amount of prayer or tears was going to bring him back. My entire family was devastated by our loss. I don't believe my father ever fully recovered. If anything, it made him care less about himself and his family, if that was even possible.

For the most part, my parents were nonexistent in our lives, so I was Rico's guardian and protector, especially in the streets. I spent a lot of my youth trying to protect Ricardo and myself from bullies who seemed to inhabit every street corner in the Bronx. The problem was that my brother wasn't a street kid, he wasn't a tough kid, and he wasn't a bully—he was goofy, innocent, and very shy, I think mostly because of his weight problems. Rico was always a huge kid—a behemoth compared to the other kids in the neighborhood. He might have been just seven or eight years old, but he easily looked like he was 13 or 14 years old because of his size and that got us both into a lot of trouble.

One of the first street fights I recall was in the third grade. I was coming home from Catholic school with one of my friends, Joey Adams, one of the toughest Irish kids I had ever met, when someone ran up to me and said, "Yo, your brother is getting beat down in the schoolyard!" As Joey and I ran into they yard, I could see these two little black kids who barely came up to Rico's armpits slapping the shit out of him. They were so short they had to jump up to hit him in the face but that didn't stop them.

I got right in there, throwing punches to defend him. Much to my surprise Joey didn't jump in to help me out; shit, I guess he wasn't as tough as I thought he was. When I turned around to see where Rico was, I barely made out the soles of his shoes as he ran out of the schoolyard. It was at that moment that I realized I would be alone in the streets and that despite this I would always have the heart to rescue my brother from any fight.

I lost the fight that day. More accurately, I got the living shit kicked out of me, but I felt good about what I had done for my brother. I got my blows in there and was headed home to face the real beef, the beef with my mother and father, over the ripped and bloodied Catholic school uniform that was going to cost my mother a small fortune to replace. Anyone who ever went to Catholic school knows those blazers weren't cheap, so I'd have to take another beating when I reached the apartment.

When I got home my mother asked me what the hell happened to me, meaning what the hell happened to my uniform. I told her I had gotten into a fight and just as I had predicted, my mother pounced on me and started giving me a boxing lesson of her own. All I could do was cover up my face. When I looked up I saw my father coming to join the fracas. *Fuck me...Here we go!*

My father, who hadn't spent a dime to buy my uniform, joined right in. After a few blows I screamed out, "I did it to protect Ricardo!" Surprisingly, my father stopped dead in his tracks and looked at me with both pride and confusion. I explained that they were beating up on Ricardo and that I had no choice but to defend my brother, hell, to defend my family name, in the streets. Hearing this, my father started to walk away in search of Rico. When he got a hold of my brother, he almost beat him to death. I began to feel bad for him but, shit, he did leave me there to get my ass kicked. I couldn't be the only one getting beat down today.

A few years later I wouldn't have to worry about getting my Catholic school blazer messed up in a fight ever again, as my mother's hopes of a Catholic school education for her boy went up in flames. A lot of my trouble in the early years derived from being a Latino kid in a predominantly white neighborhood. Economically we were probably the poorest family in the neighborhood, but culturally we were rich beyond our means. My earliest friends were Irish, African American, Turkish, Greek, and Armenian. I remember going to my Turkish friend Ali's house and eating his mother's fresh baked bread, dipped in oil and spread with olives, while all of my friends would come over and eat white rice and black beans at my house. I grew up with friends from all walks of life. I have never judged a person because of their race or background and it has always been hard for me to maintain family ties or friendships with people who do.

To me racism is the ugliest form of human expression. When I was young, I was shitted on for being Latino and poor. Then I wasn't Puerto Rican enough because I was half Cuban, or not Cuban enough because I was half Puerto Rican. I had been hearing "spic" all my life but it became worse when I starting going to an almost all-white Catholic school. No matter how hard my mother worked to send us there, the kids would always treat us like if we were on welfare.

In school, being called a spic automatically became a challenge to a duel. At the time I was too young to understand what all the biases were about; I just knew that if you messed with me, I was going to give it right back to you. One afternoon a few white boys decided to start with me in the school hallway. As soon as one of the white boys got within striking distance I pulled out the 007 knife my cousin Cano had given me after I had gotten into some trouble around my way.

So there I was in the hallway, brandishing my knife. It was the first time I had pulled it on anyone and I made sure they saw what I was holding. A few of the boys ran off immediately but I had one boy backed up against a locker. I warned him, "If you ever call me a fucking spic again I will kill you." Then I backed off and let the boy go running to the nuns. Needless to say, that event ended my Catholic school education.

My only regret for being thrown out of school was the embarrassment it caused my mother and the look of pain in her eyes when she asked me why I had done it. I don't think she really understood the racism I was being subjected to at such a young age, or maybe she just didn't care. I'm sure she would have preferred that I turn the other cheek, but I just couldn't do it any longer. I was happy that her effort to bribe the priests with more tuition money wasn't successful.

When I look back now, I wish I was mature enough to make it work. My mother worked two jobs to finance our education. She ran two laundromats in the Bronx, one on Tiebout Avenue and one between Ryer and Valentine Avenues. She had to work twice as hard to provide the life she wanted for her family with absolutely no help from my father. As a slave for a small wage, my mother used what little she earned to give us the opportunity to do better in life. My mother laid the foundation, and although I wasn't ready to follow her lead at that time, I would eventually understand and come to appreciate her sacrifice.

Track Two: Into Something... Gonna Make You Move

Back in the early 1970s the Fordham Road area of the Bronx was broken up into two sections: if you were on the 183rd side of the Grand Concourse, you were most likely black or Latino and if you crossed over towards Poe Park, you were walking into a lighter side of town, the side of town infested with white gangs like the Golden Guineas, a predominantly Italian-American gang that ruled north of Fordham Road. I learned early on not to go there.

At the time, 183rd Street could have been considered a neutral ground for gangs. At any given time you would see the Royal Javelins, the Supreme Bachelors, the Golden Guineas, the Seven Immortals, the Black Assassins, the Black Spades, the Savage Skulls, the Savage Nomads and the Ghetto Brothers marching through.

Gang life was not for me because I didn't need or want anyone telling me how to live my life. I didn't need their orders or their rules. I chose to run with my boys from the block and when the time came we dubbed ourselves the East Side Boys. The difference was there was no single leader, we were all leaders, and that structure worked out a lot better for me.

While I knew some real motherfuckers who were ex-gang members, I also saw that a lot of punks joined gangs because they wanted the security of numbers. The sad thing is that they are usually the ones to start all the shit. They become the instigators of most of the beefs because they feel a sense of power when their boys are around. It's easy as hell to be tough when you outnumber someone five-to-one.

In my eyes a gang leader doesn't look to prove their power to anyone. If you know you are tough and you know you have the heart of a lion, there is no reason for you to walk around flexing your muscle. There is a lot of truth to the saying, "Real bad boys move in silence." The toughest guys I ran with back in the days were also some of the most quiet and humble men I knew. The real tough guys in my neighborhood only did what they had to do when they were provoked, to survive, to get ahead, or to protect their own.

When I was eight years old, I was into drawing, painting, and building models of ships, cars, and monsters like Dracula, Frankenstein, or the Mummy. The problem was I didn't have any money to buy my art supplies or models. A friend of my father's introduced me to the shoeshine hustle and even built me a shine box and gave me all the necessary things to start my own route. I was excited to make my own money so that I could be independent and buy my own gear or grab a slice of pizza at Susie's anytime I wanted. But I failed to realize the risks associated with owning my own business in the Bronx.

I set up shop right in front of Alexander's department store on Fordham Road, where I caught heavy foot traffic and charged a quarter for a shine. What I didn't know at the time was that I was sitting in someone else's territory. One afternoon while I was waiting for my next customer, two black guys rolled up on me. They told me not to make a sound and not to move. It was the first time I was the victim of a strong-arm robbery and when I told my cousin Cano about it, he told me I was stupid for not packing the 007 knife he had gotten me. From that day on I swore I would always be carrying and I never moved from my spot.

Not too long afterwards, four Golden Guineas approached me. I didn't wait for the guy to finish asking me what the fuck I was doing there. I just pulled my knife and started walking towards them, making sure they read in my face that I would not hesitate to stab one of them. It felt good to see the, "Oh shit!" look on their faces.

"Leave the crazy spic alone," one of the guys told his crew before they disappeared. Having a weapon in my hand gave me a sense of power that became an addiction and an obsession that would stay with me for years to come.

One afternoon after grabbing a slice at Susie's, I headed back to the block to check on my boys. As I was about to bite into my pizza, a tall Spanish older guy grabbed me from behind and put me in a chokehold while his partner, a black guy, opened his trench coat to block people from seeing what was happening. Within seconds they had snatched my baby chain, a chain with a cross that many Latino parents buy for their children when they do their first Communion.

When Cano, a Savage Skull, heard about the incident he sent out word that when he found the person that robbed his little cousin, there would be a price to pay. Being that most criminals are connected on the streets, it took Cano only a few days to find the guys. When he got them, he brought me to the schoolyard where I saw two guys from my cousin's crew holding the Spanish guy. As I walked towards the guy, Cano asked me what I was going to do. I looked my cousin in the eye and said, "What do you want me to do?"

Cano snapped back, "I want you to fuck him up. He robbed you, he disrespected you, he disrespected this family, and you have to make him pay."

I looked the guy in the face and felt more sorry for him than anything else. When I told Cano to let him go, my cousin slapped me in the face. I looked up at the Spanish guy again. He had this shitty grin on his face, looking at me as though I was a little punk. Anger began to boil within me. I pulled out my knife and I stabbed him.

Damn… I just stabbed somebody.

He let out a loud scream. I could barely feel the blade go into his body so I stabbed him again and again. Each time I stabbed him, his screams grew louder, giving me a sick sense of satisfaction. I think I took out all my years of pent up frustration on this poor guy, and eventually Cano had to pull me away so I wouldn't kill him. What surprised me most was that I felt no remorse. I felt nothing, just numbness.

After the incident I was considered a member of the Baby Skulls. I was ten years old. I tattooed an L, for my name, with India ink on my upper right arm; my introduction to gang life in the Bronx. Even though I was a member of the Baby Skulls, I didn't run with them. They were just a bunch of wild-ass little kids who were not old enough to roll with the big boys. Instead, I had my own crew, the East Side Boys.

We named ourselves the East Side Boys, after the TV series *The Bowery Boys*, and we even had our own favorite candy store that we used to hang out in every day, on 184th Street and Valentine Avenue. My East Side Boys period started around 1969. I was heavily influenced by the music of the era—the Doors, Rolling Stones, the Motown explosion, Led Zeppelin, and my favorite band, War. I remember rocking to hits like "The Cisco Kid," a favorite of gangbangers in the 70s, and "Spill the Wine," which I loved because it had a Spanish woman speaking on the background over a crazy funky phat beat.

The East Side Boys became my extended family from the ages of seven to 14. Karim was one of the oldest guys in the crew and had moved to our block a few years earlier from Bushwick, Brooklyn. He had a fascination with the mafia and mob culture, and brought that mindset to our crew. My best memories of him were of our trips to Delancey Street in the Lower East Side to buy fresh clothes and cop some matzo ball soup, potato knishes, and hot pastrami on rye from Katz's Deli. His brother Tony Rome was just as crazy as me. Then we had the three brothers, Tony, Eddie, and Benny Sunshine, who were down for anything—and of course there was my oldest friend from the crew, Joey Adams, his brother Pat, my friend George, and Robert who we called Chino.

There was also my boy Josh and his cousin Pierre who were being raised by their grandmother from St. Lucia who made the best apple pie I ever had in my life. I first met Josh in the schoolyard of Elizabeth Barrett Baron when we got into a fistfight, which ended with me snatching a stickball bat from Karim and knocking Josh the fuck out, leaving behind two permanent lumps on his forehead. The stickball bat incident was a result of him punching me in the balls during our fight. From then on he went by the name Lumpy, which he hated. Over the years we became real tight friends.

I can't forget about my boy Papo—we became like brothers. His mother died in a Bronx apartment fire in the early 70s and from then on he just didn't give a fuck about anyone or anything. He would mutilate his arms with a 007 knife and I picked up the game of cutting myself from hanging out with him. I was just so numb from all of the shit happening to me that the only way I could feel alive was to feel the pain of a blade slicing into my arm or to punch out windows in the hallways of buildings around the neighborhood. We must have gone to the hospital together at least a half a dozen times. He never gave a fuck about dying; he was the realest dude in our crew.

In the beginning we were into everyday type trouble, the same shit all inner-city youth get into when there are no programs, no camps, and no after-school activities. I remember there was a General Electric warehouse on 184th and Fields Place, right across the street from my house. The rocket scientists who worked there would discard the old fluorescent light bulbs right in front of the warehouse, which we scooped up by the box-load before taking them to the roofs of buildings facing the Grand Concourse. Why no one ever questioned ten teenage boys running up the steps of their buildings, laughing loudly, and carrying as many light bulbs as we could, is beyond me.

Let the games begin…

Call it the Bronx Olympics, if you will, as the East Side Boys and I had honed our tossing skills launching light bulb after light bulb down onto the street six stories below. No one was safe. We aimed at pedestrians, cars, buses, and delivery trucks. We would throw fast, then get the hell out of there. I'm sure if we had ever been caught, we would have been thrown off the roof ourselves.

The Grand Concourse originally named the Grand Boulevard and Concourse was actually modeled after a famous street in Paris called the Champs-Élysées. Construction began on the Grand Concourse in 1889 and it officially opened in 1909—and here we were some 60 years later turning this road into our own private amusement park for the thrill of a laugh and teenage mischief.

At this early stage in our criminal careers, although we were far from the worst the Bronx had to offer, we proved to be a definite nuisance to the neighborhood. When the East Side Boys weren't throwing shit off of rooftops and getting into fights with other neighborhood crews, we used to sneak into the RKO, Loews Paradise, the Capri Theatre, the Art Jerome, and the Valentine Theatre. We played basketball, softball, and stickball all the time. We never really cut class, but if we did, we would do it together and sneak off to the movies to catch the latest kung fu or blaxploitation flick like *5 Fingers of Death*, *The Chinese Connection*, *Fist of Fury*, *Return of the Dragon*, *Enter the Dragon*, *Superfly*, *Shaft*, *Cleopatra Jones*, *Truck Turner*, and *Dolomite*. We were just restless kids looking for stuff to get into to occupy our time.

The East Side Boys were like family to me while my own family took a turn for the worse. In 1972, when I was 11 years old, my mother was diagnosed with breast cancer. To spare us the stress of seeing my mother battle for her life, we were shipped off to Miami to live with her brother's family. It was there that I would be introduced to the family with money, manners, and morals.

In Florida we stayed with my Uncle Candido, Aunt Lola, and their four sons Diego, Alberto, Candido Jr., and Eric at their house in Coral Gables. My brother and I were made to feel like outsiders from the jump. I'm not sure why they harbored ill feelings towards my brother and me. It could be due to the fact that my mother married a Puerto Rican man, or because we were rough kids who had grown up a hell of a lot less fortunate than their children, but whatever the reason, I knew we weren't welcome there. They acted as though they were better than everyone else. They were racist against black people and that was something that definitely rubbed me the wrong way. I had a lot of black friends back in the Bronx and to hear them talking about black people the way they did was something that only made me dislike them even more.

At the same time, living with them showed me what life was supposed to look like. In the Bronx there weren't very many rules, but in Miami I was exposed to discipline, structure, and success. I saw what it was like for Latinos to own cars, homes, and businesses. I learned about the value of money and what it was like to make an honest dollar for an honest day's work. Candido owned a Texaco station where I pumped gas, checked oil gauges, stocked shelves, and cleaned up around the place. Alberto had a department store with a small café that served sánwiches Cubano, café Cubano, and pastelitos; I worked there as well. My other uncle Mario had a construction company and uncle Juanito ran a car dealership. I also went to a bilingual school where the teachers catered to Latino kids, in direct contrast to all the racism and discrimination I had faced earlier in the Catholic school system. It was a huge contrast to my life in the Bronx. Somewhere deep down inside I knew that my life in New York was fucked up and I'd be lying if I said I didn't dream of staying in Miami. I loved it there.

I was beginning to grow accustomed to my new standard of living—but I don't think the life was becoming accustomed to me. I always knew how to find trouble. My cousins had introduced me to hunting, which was something my family was very involved in out in Miami. Someone should have told them about my weapon obsession. They should have known better than to show me a gun, but I guess they thought I'd stick to their rules, that is, not to play with the guns in the house.

Regardless of their wishes, I had grown accustomed to playing with the shotgun in the house and handling the weapon when no one was around. I would load and unload the weapon, aim it around the room, and pretend I was getting ready to let off a shot. One afternoon I decided to pull the trigger right after I loaded the gun.

BOOM

The bullet went straight through three rooms in the house—and in the last room was my five-year-old cousin, Eric. My hands shook as I got up to go check on everyone. When the shotgun went off, the first question to race through my mind was if I had just killed someone in my family. The next question was what would the consequences be for shooting up my family's home. I had no idea what the price would be, but I figured it would be more severe than coming home with a torn up Catholic school blazer.

My hands shook as I got up to check on everyone. I walked out of the bedroom and into one of the biggest ass whippings of my life. They didn't wait to take turns—they all jumped me at the same time and beat the living shit out of me while shouting at me that I could have fucking killed someone. I think it was the first time I ever heard my better-than-you family ever use a curse word.

It was time for me to go home.

My family in Florida never really helped my mother with her illness. My mother was the baby girl of her family and she was sick for many years. Sure they took Rico and me in, but they didn't exactly make our stay easy. With all of their wealth and power, they never once reached out to my mother financially. I recall my mother asking for financial assistance and they always made her feel like shit about it. What they had in wealth they lacked in compassion. No one ever expected her to survive her bout with cancer, but she did.

While I was in Miami, I believed that we would never see my mother alive again. I spent untold hours waiting for the call to come, telling us that my mother had passed away. Before leaving the Bronx I remember overhearing that my mother had six months to live, yet we had been in Miami over a year. I had accepted the fact that she was going to die and that I would never see her again. The phone finally did ring one day, and much to my elated surprise I was told my mother had beaten the disease. I couldn't have been any happier—she was still with us.

It was surreal to return to that apartment in the Bronx after having lived like a king in Miami, but it felt more like home than Florida ever could. It was like heaven to me. Hugging my mother for the first time in a year and a half was like being born again. My mother's voice was like music to my soul but it became apparent pretty quickly that the cancer had damaged her both physically and mentally. Prior to being stricken with cancer my mother was the classic comedian. Hearing my mother laugh always filled my heart with joy and always gave me the comfort of knowing things were going to be okay, but after her battle with cancer she rarely found the energy to muster up a laugh. It was as if the cancer had stripped my mother of her spirit; her love of life and laughter no longer filled the room. She was not the strong woman I had known, she was still recovering from her treatments, and mostly bed-ridden when I got back home. For the first time in my life I truly felt alone.

One day not long after we returned, I heard a woman screaming as I made the way up the steps of my building towards our fourth-floor apartment. By the time I hit the second floor, I knew the woman screaming was my mother. I rushed up to my door, my hands shaking as I tried to get inside the apartment, afraid a burglar had entered and was raping my mother. I burst into the apartment only to discover my father beating my mother in the bedroom.

This motherfucker.

An intense anger, an uncontrollable rage, immediately overcame me. I couldn't believe what I was seeing. This piece of shit was beating a woman who just had a breast removed, a woman whose body had been ravaged by radiation and chemotherapy. A woman who was a mere shell of her old self, who rarely left our home, and was at his complete and total mercy.

Up until that moment I had always been able to control my anger at my father when he beat my mother, because I felt too small to rescue her from his punishing hand, as well as out of fear of what he might do to me. But I could no longer sit by and watch this evil person attack my mother, especially not after what she had just been through.

Before entering the bedroom, I went into the kitchen to grab a knife. Not just any knife, but the biggest fucking knife I could find. There was no time to think about whether or not I was going to plunge this knife into my father's body as I raced into the room. I only knew I had to do something to save my mother from the hands of the person brutalizing her.

"Get your fucking hands off my mother before I fucking kill you mother-fucker," I said as placed the knife to his throat. Had he made a move, I would have sliced his throat right then and there. As my mother screamed at me to put the knife down, I commanded my father, "Get the fuck out of this house or I am going to kill you."

With the knife still pressed against his throat, I walked my father towards the front door of our apartment and slammed it shut when he exited. Then I let out the biggest breath of air I had ever held in my life.

Although my mother and I didn't talk about the incident, it didn't take long for my aunts to come upstairs and raise all kinds of hell. I told them to go fuck themselves. They knew how long my father had been beating us, and they never did anything about it. As far I was concerned, they could go straight to hell and take my father with them. I had no remorse. In fact, I was damn proud of my actions that day. I finally felt like a man, and in my mind I was prepared for the repercussions. At least my father now understood that I would no longer sit by and watch him beat my mother.

After a week had passed and things seemed to be dying down, I let my guard down. After school one afternoon, I was sitting on the steps in the lobby of my building talking to a friend when my father appeared. He was staring me up and down like he wanted to fight and I had no way to escape the lobby. My father started asking me one question after the other. What was I doing there? Why wasn't I in school? Did I do my homework? Why was I hanging out in the street like a *títere*, (hoodlum)?

Before I ever saw it coming, he sucker punched me.

Fade to black.

I woke up in Fordham Hospital, the same hospital in which I was born. The man who helped bring me into this world had tried to take me out. It took a little while to get my bearings, and I wondered why cops were standing over me. They questioned me, then the hospital administrators and social services people had questions of their own. I told them all the same thing, "My father punched me." It was the only thing I could remember.

When I saw myself for the first time in a mirror, I couldn't believe what I saw; I went into shock and couldn't stop crying. I looked like the fucking Elephant Man. My head was the size of a basketball and my left eye was swollen shut. Black, purple, and dark red were the new colors of my face. When my father punched me, my face hit the concrete wall of the building so hard that the impact almost knocked my eyeball out. That single punch caused me massive damage and multiple surgeries. To this day the scars are still visible.

I spent a month and a half in the hospital recovering from my injuries. I was told I was fortunate not to have lost an eye. However, I did lose a father that day, and I lost the possibility that he would right all the wrongs he had done over the years. My father would go on to serve one month in prison for his attack on me, but the true justice was in the fact that he never spent another night under the same roof with us again. This was one time my mother wouldn't forgive him, and with a restraining order against him, we'd never have to deal with the hands of that monster again.

I was now head of the household, free to involve myself in any and all criminal activities I saw fit. It's not so much that I wanted to be a criminal, but I had long since learned if I wanted anything, I had to get it myself. Someone once asked me if I got my toughness from my father. The answer was no. The streets made me tough. I had to deal with so much bullshit growing up that I had no choice but to be tough. Out of that toughness came my lack of compassion. The coldness in my heart was a direct result of the harsh reality that I knew my life to be, making me the first in my neighborhood to hit someone with a baseball bat, to stab, or even shoot someone if necessary. My father did give me one thing: his barbarian-like behavior. The only difference between him and I was that I used my barbarian nature to survive, he used his to torture.

It wouldn't take long for me to use my newfound toughness to build a reputation for the East Side Boys. The elders who ran the social clubs and the bodegas took notice and when they needed a message sent they would often call on us. They were messages that were always written in blood. The first *bodegero* (bodega owner) to hire us for a job was an older gentleman named Eddie. Eddie told us that he had a feeling his wife might be fucking around with a guy over on Tiebout Avenue so he sent Tony Rome and me over to the building to hang out on the stoop and check things out. It took us just two days to catch Eddie's wife messing around. I felt a little bad about telling him that his wife was fucking around with another dude. Shit, that was the same reason Mario had killed himself and I worried that maybe Eddie would follow suit.

Instead, Eddie offered Tony and me a hundred dollars each to beat the shit out of the guy who was sleeping with his wife. The next day we waited for the guy to come walking down Tiebout Avenue. When we spotted him, we started walking right towards him. Just as he started to pass us Tony said, "What the fuck did you just say to me?"

Before the guy could say one word, Tony snuffed him and I followed suit with a flurry of punches to the guys face and head. Once he was down, we started kicking and stomping the shit out of him. The poor bastard tried to ask us who the hell we were and what we wanted. "Take my wallet!" he screamed as we continued to beat him. I didn't give a shit. It was a job, and at that time for one hundred dollars I would have beat down just about anyone. This was our way of making a name for ourselves in the neighborhood and ensuring that more jobs followed. It was the beginning of many beatings for hire, and there was no looking back now.

Eventually the small crimes turned to bigger crimes, until our crew was nothing less than a full-fledged criminal enterprise. Running with the East Side Boys, I was arrested half a dozen times before I was fifteen years old, but no arrest was ever serious enough to make me want to stop. After I was arrested for the first time, the rest came very easy. Most people probably experienced a sense of fear the first time those handcuffs were slapped on. For me it was a necessary step in the streets towards gaining the respect of my peers in the neighborhood.

One day someone in the crew came back to the neighborhood with news that a department store on Fordham Road had partially burned down. The fire at Robin's meant easy access from the roof into the fashionable clothing store, so a quick plan was hatched and we took off to pull our first real heist

As we cased the joint, we discovered that the fire had left a gaping hole in the side of the building connecting Robin's to a Salsa record shop, and the best they had done was patch it up with a few pieces of plywood. In a few minutes we had ripped the plywood from the wall. I was chosen to be the lookout on the roof while Tony Rome, Karim, and Josh climbed through the hole and into the store.

We had brought along a bunch of heavy-duty trash bags; the guys inside were packing the bags as fast as they could and then passing them out to me, one after another. After about a half an hour of this, as I turned to put the bag down, someone reached out and took it from me.

Oh shit! Who the fuck did I just pass that bag to? raced through my mind as I slowly turned to look.

Standing there were the detectives who had questioned us earlier about some other shit we had done in the neighborhood. They wouldn't be asking me many questions this time—after all, I had just handed him a garbage bag full of stolen clothing. I wasn't sure whether to laugh or cry so I just shook my head in shock.

As the detectives handcuffed us and marched us in front of the crowd that had gathered on Fordham Road, I felt a weird sense of pride. The East Side Boys had just made a name for themselves in the robbery game. As we were placed into the squad cars headed to the 46th Precinct, we all had shitty little grins on our faces. It was like an initiation and it felt cool to be arrested. I held my head up high knowing I had just gained more power and respect in my neighborhood.

Track Three: Here We Come… On The Run

If life taught me anything through my first fourteen or so years, it was simply not to ever get comfortable with my existence in this world. Any time I thought things were looking up, something would happen to smack me right back down to reality. I'm not sure how bad I was in my previous life but if you believe in that sort of thing, karma was surely kicking the shit out of me this go around. I got tired of trying to figure out, "Why me?"

In 1974, I was in my final year at Creston Junior High School on 181st Street. While I was sitting in class about a year after my father attacked me, the dean came in and asked to speak to me. I scrolled through the list of things that could possibly get me in trouble, but this time something was different. The dean's demeanor made me think I was about to receive bad news about my mother. A stream of tears began falling down my face. When we reached the office, he told me my grandmother Virginia was on the phone and asked me to sit down. I went numb. Something inside of me told me I was about to receive the news I waited for so many times before, while living in Miami. I couldn't believe she was finally gone.

With tears streaming down my face, I took the phone and braced myself. My grandmother whispered through the phone receiver, *"Mi hijo, tu papá está muerto."*

What the fuck?

I let out a huge sigh and I hung up the phone. I tried to register what she had said.

My father was dead.

Fuck that dude.

For all his years of alcohol abuse, he suffered from cirrhosis of the liver and earned a one-way ticket to eternal sleep. My mother didn't attend the funeral, and if I had it my way, I wouldn't have been there either. People in my family thought I was cold because I displayed no emotion. I had no tears left in me for the person who had tried to destroy my family, the person who was fortunate enough to die peacefully. That chapter of my life closed when the casket dropped. I felt no sorrow, no remorse, and no sense of loss. I felt nothing.

When my father died we moved to 2385 Valentine Avenue. My mother, who was still recovering from cancer and out of work, had no choice but to go on welfare. It was really tough for us as a family, but we always kept it moving, and my mother always managed to keep her sense of humor, despite the circumstances.

There was a family that lived in a private house across the street from our building and the father used to get stupid drunk on the weekends. He would stand in the street yelling at people. I used to shut off the light in my bedroom and crack my window open about an inch so I could yell all kinds of shit back at him, while also repeating everything he said. Man! He would go nuts screaming, "Who's that? I'll fucking kill you! Show your face motherfucker!" Rico and I would die laughing, while my mother used to tell me all the time that he was my real father. When I was born they used to switch the babies in the maternity ward and my mother was sure to remind me of this. She would say, "Come on Albertico, that's not nice, leave your father alone and stop bothering him."

Although we were poor, my mother somehow managed to open a line of credit with the bodega on the corner of 184th Street, which she used to pay with her bi-weekly welfare checks. One day in 1975 I came home from school with my boy Papo, entered the apartment, and found my mother crying uncontrollably. She didn't want to tell me what happened and locked herself in her bedroom. As I was leaving, a downstairs neighbor asked me, "Did you hear what happened to your mother today?"

Apparently Andre, the owner of the bodega, had put on a show, screaming and embarrassing my mother in front of everyone in the store, saying that she could no longer get any credit until she brought her tab up to date. He went on to say that if she didn't have any money, now that my father was dead, she should find a new husband.

When I heard this I grabbed my .25 automatic burner and set out to smoke this motherfucker, but Papo took it from me and said, "Nah bro, you don't need to shoot this dude. He's a fucking old man. Let's just go fuck him up."

I grabbed a pipe from my room and made my way to the corner store but he wasn't there. One of the clerks told us that he was at the laundromat down the block. The poor bastard never saw us coming. I cracked him in the head with the pipe as Papo pulled out my pistol and screamed at everyone to get the fuck out. Andre hit the ground and I continued to wail on him while he begged for his life. After a few minutes of beating him senseless we took off running because someone yelled that the cops were on their way.

I later found out that I broke his arm in a few places, his cheekbone, and six ribs and put him in the hospital for a week. The block got hot for me, so I hid in Papo's house until things calmed down. My homeboys also paid Andre's son a visit and told him that if they pressed charges against me the store would be burnt down with them still in it. As word got around about what Andre did to my mother, people stopped going to that store and less than a year later they sold it.

Shortly after my father's death, a friend introduced me to Curtis Fisher, who had just lost his father as well. Although I didn't know anything about the guy, his welcoming personality made me comfortable around him right away. Curt was one of those guys you meet and you automatically know you're going to be friends with for a long time to come. The first time I met him he greeted me with a huge smile and said, "Paul told me a lot of good things about you man." I let him know I had also heard a lot of good things about him and before I knew it, we were hanging out together on a daily basis.

It didn't take me long to find out that Curt already had a reputation of his own. He went by the name "Doc" because of his nasty finger rolls, love for basketball, and Julius "Dr J" Erving. He was also a real laid-back brother—funny, articulate, very smart, and in the neighborhood he was known as a fly guy for the way he dressed. When you saw us together, you always saw two fly cats dressed alike with the Kangol hats, the suede Pumas, Pro-Keds, overlaps, AJs, Lee jeans, and mock neck shirts. We were all about looking fly at all times. Our collection of gear was sick—you couldn't even walk into my room on Valentine Avenue; I had Kangols and sneakers in every color to match my outfits. Curt and I used to go down and dig on Delancey Street for the latest clothes just as hard as we would soon do for our rare records. It was just that serious.

A student of urban culture, Curt had a profound and deep understanding of street life and was already getting involved in the early stages of the Hip Hop movement. Hip Hop in the early 70s was entirely word of mouth. The earliest parties were thrown by DJ Kool Herc, who threw a back-to-school party with his sister Cindy on August 11, 1973, which has since been dated as the birth of Hip Hop.

While growing up in Kingston, Jamaica, Herc saw and heard the sound systems at dancehall parties, where MCs, known there as toasters, would get on the mic to accompany the DJ. When Herc moved to the Bronx, he brought these ideas with him. His first sound system consisted of two turntables and a guitar amp on which he would play records like James Brown's "Give It Up or Turnit a Loose," the Jimmy Castor Bunch's "It's Just Begun," and Booker T. & the MG's "Melting Pot." With Bronx clubs afflicted by the menacing presence of street gangs, uptown

DJs playing for an older disco crowd, and commercial radio catering to a different demographic, Herc's parties had ready-made audiences. His reputation was huge way before I ever had the chance to see him.

I went to my first Kool Herc jam in 1974, when I was 13 years old. He was doing a warm-up at the Webster P.A.L., where I used to box. I was training very hard to become a great fighter, throwing all of my aggression into the ring, with aspirations of one day boxing in the Olympics. My idol and hero was Roberto Duran, who fought his way out of the deadly slums of Panama to become the Lightweight Champion of the World.

One day, while hitting the heavy bag in the gym downstairs at the P.A.L., I heard loud music blaring above me. As I walked up the steps, the music grew louder and louder. I entered the larger gym and saw two columns of speakers on each side of the stage. The speakers were so huge they looked like they were kissing the ceiling. I asked someone what was going on and they told me Kool Herc was throwing a jam at the center that night. Damn! Herc was already a legend in the Bronx and when the dude told me that he was standing right there on stage, I just walked right up in front, stood there in my boxing gear, and stared in amazement as he put one record after another onto the turntables in a process that never seemed to stop. The music I heard that day put me into a trance, and when Herc picked up the microphone to say a simple, "Check one and two"—that was it for me.

At the time Curt went by Casanova Fly, or Caz, and people were calling me LOU 183, which was my graffiti tag. My friend Karim from the East Side Boys used to write MICO and got me into graffiti when I first came back from Miami. He was the first dude to show me a black book. It was really easy for me to get into it because I was drawing, sketching, and painting for as far back as my memory served me. Most of the East Side Boys wrote graffiti, and we bombed everything in sight. The trains were rolling canvasses with tags and burners. In my neighborhood, graf legend STAY HIGH 149 was king.

Back in the 70s graffiti was very political. It became a way for us to send a message to the rest of the world, to let them know we had been abandoned by the dirty politicians and the corrupt system. Shit, even President Ford told New York City to drop dead. We were left for dead by the rest of the country but the resilience of a bunch of teenagers trying to find a way to make life work birthed Hip Hop, a movement that has since become a way of life for people around the globe.

Caz and I both liked to battle b-boys at the jams. Although we didn't get deeply into breakin', we enjoyed rocking parties to pass the time. At the time, breakin' was really new so the jams were always mixed with people doing the hustle and shit like that. Caz was the tall, lanky, smooth type brother so he could hustle his ass off. I had a few up-rock moves, and then I would hit the floor pretty quickly, but on the real, we mostly got our clothes dirty, which was something I never liked. Needless to say, our b-boy careers were very short lived.

We quickly turned our attention to the DJ. Music was the party, and the party revolved around whoever was playing the music. We both wanted to be the center of attention and decided to become DJs ourselves. The DJ movement was very fresh in those early days and Caz and I had to find our own way, our own space, and our own rules. In the beginning we fucked around with whatever house equipment we had. I would sometimes steal my mother's turntable and take it over to Caz's house. We would play two records at the same time, turn up the volume on one player while turning the volume down on the next to blend, mix, and emulate what we saw Kool Herc doing with a real mixer and sound system. We would play the hottest tunes of the time from the Tramps, the Commodores, James Brown, Curtis Mayfield, Kool and the Gang, the Ohio Players, and the Jimmy Castor Bunch.

DJing was a great distraction from the streets and it felt good to have found something productive in my life. It was worlds apart from running the streets with the East Side Boys and it made me feel like I had something to offer this world. Little by little, I tried to pull myself out of the streets and to disassociate myself with the thugs in my neighborhood. I just began spending as much time as possible around Caz. He and I became like brothers and a big part of that was because we had both lost a lot in our short time on earth. It connected us and allowed us to grow a strong bond as we spent countless hours talking about the histories of our families, who our fathers were, and how we felt about the loss. Our friendship forced me to look beyond my block and at the bigger picture.

We both used a lot of comedy to mask the pain we had inside of us. We were avid collectors of records like Richard Pryor, Dick Gregory, Redd Foxx, and Bill Cosby. If Caz didn't care so much about Hip Hop, he definitely could have had a future in comedy, because he was one of the funniest people I had ever met. Caz was a natural comedian who would rip a motherfucker apart with his snapping abilities. He took me back to my childhood when my mother used to make me laugh all the time with her comic routines. If we weren't talking about comedy, we were talking about fashion, music, the last jam Herc threw, or dreaming about what we wanted to do with our lives. We spent a lot of time talking about how we were going to be the next Kool Herc. There weren't a lot of DJs in the neighborhoods, so if we could find a way to get some equipment of our own, we'd be able to emulate what we saw him do and become the next big DJs in the neighborhood. Caz was the one who had a real vision for Hip Hop. I had not yet been fully converted until the day he told me how serious he was about starting a DJ crew with me. He had hatched a scheme to get his mother to allow him to purchase real DJ equipment with money his father had left behind when he passed away.

What the fuck? Your father left you money when he passed away?

Caz was spending a lot of time trying to convince his mother that it would be a good investment into his future and that it would keep him out of the streets. "Yo Lou, if we get this money we can really get this shit jumping off," Caz told me. I always appreciated the way he said "we," like I had anything to do with raising the money to get us started.

It's not like today, where a kid would be able to tell his mother, "Mom I want to be like Puffy. I want to be like Jay-Z." At that time there was no blueprint for this, no possible way of making a comparison to what it was we were trying to accomplish. The fact that Caz was able to convince his mother to use some of his inheritance money, his college money, on DJ equipment was yet another testament to not only how verbally gifted this kid was, but also how passionate he was about the whole movement.

I'll never forget the day that Caz called and said, "Yo Lou, get over to my crib now, I have to show you something." I only lived a few blocks away. As I walked over, I remember thinking to myself, "No fucking way he got his mother to cave and buy him equipment," but when I got to the apartment Caz had a huge cheeseburger smile on his face.

When I laid eyes on the new equipment all I could think was *Wow—brand new equipment!* I could smell the new plastic on the two Kenwood belt drive turntables with wood molding, a no-brand mixer, and two column speakers with two ten-inch woofers and a single tweeter on both. We would later expand our system to include two 15-inch bass bottom speakers from Broman's on Fordham Road, two 12-inch horns that we stole from the 183rd Street subway station (thanks MTA!), two homemade tweeter boxes with six tweeters screwed into a couple of plywood boards, and of course our famous Clubman 2 mixer that Caz would cop during the 1977 blackout. As time went on, we would blow out our amps and speakers and break countless needles. This was one of the main reasons we started to expand our crew, the Mighty Force Crew (founded in 1977), to include DJ Mighty Mike and Starski, who would provide back-up amps, speakers, and microphones while

Whipper Whip, Dotta Rock, Mr. T, Kool Kev, and the only female of the crew, a high school girlfriend of mine Pambaataa, who we taught how to DJ. These additions added more depth, resources, and manpower to keep it moving.

But that was way into the future. It was on this day, when I was at Caz's looking at our first set of professional equipment, that it had just begun. While mixing "Apache," "Bongo Rock," "It's Just Begun," "Son of Scorpio," "Scratching," "Catch a Groove" and "I Can't Stop," I became a true convert to Hip Hop. The feeling I got from being able to throw two copies of the same record on and fade the records back and forth, to fade them in and out using an actual mixer, was like nothing I had ever experienced. It's like being a one-man band and having total control over the music. I could pick a break, a favorite part of a record, or a hook and run it back, over and over again. It gave me a feeling of total freedom, and to this day, it sends chills down my spine when I blend two records seamlessly together. For me there is no feeling in this world like rocking a party and being behind the ones and twos. It never gets old.

"Yo Lou, this shit is for real now, man," Caz said. "I want you to be my partner and I want you to be real about this." I just smiled and gave Caz a big hug as he said, "We're about to throw our first jam." DJ Louie Lou and DJ Casanova Fly were now an official DJ team and we were about to show the world our skills. We never looked back.

In order to understand how monumental this moment in history was, you have to understand that the Bronx was a totally segregated place in the 1970s. Blacks and Latinos were not united, so not only were Caz and I about to become pioneers of the Hip Hop game, we were becoming pioneers in our own neighborhoods. People weren't used to seeing a Spanish guy rolling with only black guys and rocking the turntables, but as time went along I made a name for myself and gained the respect of my peers. We were showing people that it was all right for Blacks and Latinos to share a bond of brotherhood and we both took a lot of shit for it.

At the same time, on the other side of the Bronx, the Godfather of Hip Hop, Afrika Bambaataa, was preaching the unity of black and brown. He was preaching peace, love, unity, and having fun. We were all oppressed people in the same situation, stuck in the lawlessness of the Bronx, and the real enemies damn sure weren't the cats in our neighborhoods. While no one would have bet on us to make it out, we bet on ourselves.

Practicing with Caz on the turntables was like being in boot camp. We weren't in his apartment just playing records; we were practicing routines, learning how to take our skills to the next level. One of the first things I learned to do was cut a record on time, allowing for one continuous beat so the DJ didn't interrupt the flow of the b-boys and b-girls on the dance floor. If you broke the beat you stopped the dancers in their tracks, causing them to lose their rhythms. Using the break of the record was something we had witnessed Kool Herc and Afrika Bambaataa doing. Eventually, extending the break, (the part of the record that was just music and no lyrics), later allowed the MCs to rock the party using a microphone, but in the beginning it was all about the DJ and the breakers rocking the floors. In between the breaks we would throw in Richard Pryor sound bites like, "Ah, nigga shit," "I told you boy," and "Kiss my ass, motherfucker." We weren't out there just playing one record after the other. We were elevating the art form of DJing to get a rise out of the crowd.

DJing has always been an evolutionary process. It started out very primitively by just playing popular funk joints. Then it progressed to playing two records at the same time, messing with the break, adding special effects or sound bites, blending two records to sound like one, and eventually all the cutting and scratching that became synonymous with Hip Hop music.

The more I began DJing, the more I began to find my own style and relate back to my ancestry from Puerto Rico and Cuba. I began to use the drumbeats and found that I could make my own rhythms by manipulating certain records. It was something that was in my soul the entire time, and eventually I found my own style; one geared towards the b-boys, so they could rock the party all night long. I became a battle style DJ and all around beat junkie. The beat gave me my adrenaline rush. It was that beat that made me fall in love with Hip Hop.

After about a week of practicing at Caz's crib, we were ready to throw our first real party. We loaded up all the equipment on a few dollies and we headed for Slattery Park on 183rd Street. The park occupied half a city block and was covered in concrete, with two handball courts, a set of swings, a dull basketball court, and a public swimming pool. It was during the summer of 1975 when Caz and I set up our sound system and launched our first park jam, ready to rock for the thirty or forty lucky motherfuckers that showed up. I definitely felt like a star out there rocking the wheels of steel. People loved the music and the cops never bothered us even though our equipment was plugged into a street lamp. Back in those days the NYPD had much worse crimes to worry about than a few kids jacking music from a lamppost.

At the time there weren't a lot of park jams, but we always heard stories about stick-up kids rolling up in the parks and stealing people's equipment. We never really had to deal with that bullshit, maybe because we already had street credibility. Either way, our events never had a lot of beefs, shootings, or stickups. Other than dealing with the neighborhood drug dealers who never wanted us there, we pretty much ruled our parks the same way we ruled the streets surrounding our neighborhoods.

You had different levels of people at the jams. There were b-boys and b-girls mixing it up on the dance floor, stick-up kids looking for prey, dudes looking to hook up with girls, and gangbangers looking really out of place, because by this time the street gangs had been all but shutdown in the city. Most of them traded in their Lee jackets and joined crews. Back then Hip Hop was only in the Bronx, but once people started traveling from all over the city to see the jams, the word of what was happening traveled back with them.

We would promote our shows using flyers that Caz meticulously designed. Once he was finished creating the artwork, we would take it to a printing shop on the Grand Concourse and Fordham Road, where they were hand-printed on a retro graph machine. Promoting was a lot of fun; we would hand out our flyers everywhere we went—at schools, parks, centers, buses, and trains, but mostly at other peoples' jams. We'd also get a lot of girls' phone numbers in the process, making it that much more rewarding.

But no matter where the music was taking me, it was still the Bronx at the end of the day and I was packing heat wherever I went. Of course it's the day you leave home without it that you need it the most; like the day Caz told me to roll with him to see this girl over by Roberto Clemente State Park. There was a jam going on and we decided to check it out. Caz asked me if I had my strap on me and he was surprised as hell when I told him I left it at home. "Man, we can't go into no Roberto Clemente jam without straps," Caz said. "Are you fucking crazy?"

He was right. There was an unwritten rule that you didn't go into anyone else's territory without a weapon. Caz suggested we go to the corner store to see if they had any toy guns. Better to have a fake gun than no gun at all. We bought the Starsky and Hutch set and blacked out the red tips with a black graffiti marker. Surprisingly enough the guns looked pretty damn real sticking out of our waistbands and although I didn't want to have to pull them out, it was still better than being caught with nothing more than our dicks in our hands.

About fifteen minutes after entering the park, I got into beef with some black cat that bumped into me. To make matters worse, this motherfucker did the ultimate violation: he stepped on my brand new red suede Pumas, leaving a nice dark stain on my new kicks. In those days I can't even tell you how many people got murdered over stepping on someone's new kicks. I was the only Puerto Rican in the house and I think he felt the need to test me. He probably figured I was a pussy, in his neck of the woods, and definitely outnumbered. I wasn't even with Caz when the shit happened because he had walked off to greet the DJ.

I wasn't having it, strapped or not. As the argument started to get louder and louder, I saw that eight or nine other guys were trying to surround me. I instinctively pulled up my shirt to display the handle of my toy gun. Of course, I was hoping they couldn't tell the shit was a fake. As I grabbed the handle of the gun I looked him in the eye and said, "What the fuck you want to do motherfucker? I'll blast you and your bitch-ass boys right here."

The guy immediately started crying. I guess he knew people got murdered over the type of violation he had just perpetrated on me. Caz, who finally noticed what the fuck was going on, rushed over to hold me down. When Caz reached the commotion, he put his hand on the handle of his Starsky and Hutch gun and told the crowd, "Yeah, you better back the fuck up."

As we cautiously backed away from the crowd, all we were really trying to do was find the exit door. The crowd moved with us as if trying to box us in or get close enough to snuff one of us and take our guns away. This went on for several tense moments until we found the exit, turned, and ran. The crowd loosely chased us while shouting, "If you ever come back here you motherfuckers are dead!"

Once we hit the city steps that separated Sedgwick Avenue from Roberto Clemente, Caz's gun fell out of his waistband, banged against the concrete steps, and smashed into several pieces. Caz and I busted out into laughter, realizing that our two-dollar investment most likely saved us from a severe beat down. It was these types of situations that allowed me to trust him as my right hand man; he always had my back, fake guns and all, and I had him the same way.

We ended up going back to make peace in the neighborhood. After all, we both had girls in the area, and Caz knew some of the DJ cats and we wanted to go back for future jams. It was all about the music and we were able to clear up the misunderstanding. As it turned out, the guy who had ruined my new kicks was a pretty cool guy, and the brother of a neighborhood DJ. We apologized to one another and made peace.

★ ★ ★ ★ ★

My mother was that little Spanish lady who was always sitting out the window. My mom spent so much time at that window on 2385 Valentine Avenue, our new home after my father had died, that her pillow was perfectly molded to the shape of the windowsill. To this day when I visit the old neighborhood, in my mind I can still hear my mother calling to me, *"Te veo, hijo de la gran puta"* ("I see you little motherfucker") as I tried to sneak into the building.

She, much like many nosey neighbors, was the first to invent neighborhood watch—but she only *watched*. They never really acted on anything they saw because that would have been a real violation. I mean, once in a while cops pulled up to check shit out and people suspected who placed the call, but the fact that they *never* left the windowsill made it hard to understand how they even called the cops in the first place.

While my mom didn't like me running the streets, I'm sure she lost no sleep over the fact that I could always defend myself out there. Instead she spent a lot of time watching Rico out of the window to make sure he was okay.

I remember one hot as hell summer afternoon. I was butt-naked in my bedroom getting busy with one of my little neighborhood girlfriends. Right in the middle of me doing my thing, I heard my mother screaming, *"Me tan matando mi hijo! Me tan matando tu hermano!"* which basically meant that they were killing my brother.

I jumped off my girl and opened my window to see that there were two men beating the shit out of my brother with a crowbar. I grabbed my .38 special, threw on some boxer shorts, and started making my way out of the apartment. My girlfriend was pulling at my arm screaming, "NO!" and my mother was pulling on my other arm, trying to wrestle the gun out of my hand. Eventually I let the gun go. As I passed the kitchen I saw a huge butcher knife sticking out of a chicken my mother was preparing. I grabbed the knife. With blood dripping from the blade I ran as fast as I could, barefoot with my half erect dick sticking out of my boxer shorts. As I ran across the street, I used all of that momentum to shank the shit out of him.

"Ay no me mate!" he screamed, begging me not to kill his ass as I plunged the huge knife into his back.

Oh yeah motherfucker?

I drove the knife into his back three more times. The more I stabbed him the more he screamed in pain. The more he screamed the more a crowd gathered. It must have been some scene to see a half naked teenager with his cock hanging out stabbing a full-grown man. I was hell bent on killing this motherfucker. If it weren't for John, an older guy in the neighborhood, pulling me away I would have caught my first body at that very moment. "Get the fuck out of here now," is all he said to me as he grabbed the knife right out of my hand. He ran towards his building with the evidence while I ran to my building, half naked and completely drenched in blood. It was the second time I had placed the cool steel of a knife into another man's body: the first time was to protect my family name and reputation, the second time was to protect my family.

You fuck with my family and I will fuck you up. That's all there is to it.

As my family watched this guy being loaded onto an ambulance from the windowsill, I felt nothing but justification for what I had just done. My only fear was that someone in the neighborhood would drop a dime on me, but no one ever did. In fact many people told me, "I would have done the same thing if it was my brother." I later found out that the whole incident stemmed from my brother's basketball taking a bad hop into the street and onto the hood of this guy's taxi. The driver and his buddy got out the car, picked out my brother, and decided to punish him.

While I couldn't seem to leave the streets alone, Caz and I were building names for ourselves in Hip Hop and decided it was time for a change for me. DJ Louie Lou, Lou 183, or just plain Louie was finished when Caz dubbed me DJ Disco Wiz. Although I didn't immediately take to the name, I never questioned Caz when it came to Hip Hop. He was ahead of his time, he was a visionary and a pioneer and if he said the name fit, that was it.

DJ Disco Wiz and DJ Casanova Fly were about to make our names battling other big-name DJs in the Bronx—and at the time there was no one bigger than DJ Kool Herc.

Track Four: Day or Night... Black or White

Growing up in New York improves your chances of being introduced to some of the toughest, craziest, most mentally disturbed people in the world. I don't know if there is something in the water out here, but there it no disputing the fact that the city births some of the most deranged characters life has to offer. And in my neighborhood there was no one more deranged than Francisco Mendez.

I was first introduced to Francisco when I became a member of the Baby Skulls. He was also a member, and being that we were close in age, we began running the streets together. But Francisco wasn't like the other guys I knew; there was something different about him. When I looked into his eyes I saw nothing. No emotions, no pain, no happiness. At times it felt like I was hanging out with a person who was already dead and I was careful not to get in too deep with the guy.

One afternoon we were hanging out in the schoolyard on 181st Street. Francisco grabbed a cat by the neck, poured lighter fluid all over it, and lit the poor thing on fire. Watching this cat run around the schoolyard trying to put itself out was a sickening experience even for someone who had been through as much shit as me. But what I remember to this day more than anything was the way the cat screamed as if it were a person begging to be saved, or at the very least begging to be put out of its misery. Francisco thought it was the funniest shit ever and I remember wanting to distance myself from the sick fuck from that moment on.

He always wanted to do the next crazy thing and his death wish led him to challenge anyone to anything. He was the first to want to play Russian roulette, the first to want to jump from rooftop to rooftop, the first to kill any animal he could get his hands on. The guy was just plain out of his fucking mind and I always had a gut instinct the he would find himself on the evening news for having committed a horrific crime; a crime that would shock a city that was very hard to shock.

On October, 24th, 1976 Francisco and two other men, Antonio Cordero and Hector Lopez, set a Bronx Puerto Rican social club on fire. The club was located at 1003 Morris Avenue, not too far from where we had grown up. Apparently Cordero wanted to exact revenge on his girlfriend who was out partying at the club so he had Lopez and Francisco help him set the place on fire. He didn't only want to get back at his girlfriend by slapping her around the way many Puerto Rican men did, he wanted to burn his girlfriend alive and anyone else who was unlucky enough to be inside the club that fateful night. Twenty-five people perished in the social club that night, making it one of the worst fires in New York City's history.

It was a crime that sent Francisco to jail for 25 counts of 25 years to life—not long enough if you ask me.

I remember picking up the newspaper and seeing Francisco sitting in the police car with his head down. He had just been brought back to the Bronx, from of all places Puerto Rico, where he had fled immediately after the fire to avert justice. They should have left him in PR and told the people on the island that he murdered 25 innocent Puerto Ricans including Cordero's girlfriend and her sister that night. I'm sure the people would have made sure his sentence was fitting of his crime.

Mendez, Cordero, and Lopez were sentenced in January of 1977, which was just the start of a very interesting year in New York City. The city was flat broke, cops and teachers were being laid off in record numbers, and firehouses were closing even though the Bronx alone was averaging 12,000 fires a year. Trash never seemed to be picked up in our neighborhoods. The Son of Sam was running around smoking people left and right, but if there was one thing we didn't have to worry about in the Bronx, it was the Son of Sam. He would have gotten his brains blown out had he come up to 183rd Street with that bullshit.

Ironically, this urban chaos lit the creative fires burning in so many of us. DJ Disco Wiz and DJ Casanova Fly were beginning to make our name throwing jams in our park on 183rd Street, throwing down at P.S. 123, Morris Avenue, Echo Park, Arthur Park, Roosevelt High School, and the Webster PAL. It was only a matter of time before we began to play amongst the elites. We were out to gain our respect by any means necessary. We wanted our names to be spoken in the same vein as people like Kool Herc, Afrika Bambaataa, Disco King Mario, the L Brothers, and Grandmaster Flash. To be seen as one of the best, we had to play with the best.

Our first major battle was with Kool Herc and the Herculords at the Webster PAL in early 1977. I don't think Herc wanted our show together to be billed as a battle, but we made sure it was a battle. We needed our routines to be tight because we couldn't fuck with the Herc's monster system. The night of the battle we were ready for whatever was coming our way. When we got to the spot we noticed a crowd of about 200–300 people, out of which we probably knew 20 or 30 of them. We were going to have to get busy that night if we wanted to earn the respect of a Herc crowd. What I remember the most was a real cool vibe in the crowd; there was a lot of love for us and for what we were doing. We went back and forth between our set and Herc's set all night. Caz and I were flying high. We had definitely earned our stripes that night DJing with the father of Hip Hop, as well as a lot of new fans. This was our coming out joint. This was where we belonged.

At that time, it wasn't just about playing records; as a DJ you had to have something that made you stand out. If you wanted to see some fast-ass scratching, you went to see Grandmaster Flash; if you wanted to see some ill scratching skills, you went to see Grand Wizzard Theodore; if you wanted to go listen to some real eclectic, funky beats that you never heard before, you went to see Bambaataa; and if you wanted to go hear the father rock a party, you went to see Kool Herc.

One of the first major contributions Caz and I made to Hip Hop was the creation of the first mix plate, a ten-inch demo record that was compiled of a few of our mixtapes, party tapes, pause tapes, and routine tapes combined with sound effects. The idea for a mix plate came in the lunchroom of Roosevelt High School while a white geek was listening to our mixtapes on our boombox; he suggested we make a ten-inch demo record to incorporate the sound and style we had created.

At a battle we'd throw on our plate, turn off the lights, walk away from the turntables, and rock a b-boy stance, completely fucking people's heads up. At that time no one had their own shit on wax. It was something a lot of people at the jams had never seen and it really helped elevate our game. Before the plate, you had to go to a live jam to experience a Hip Hop event; once we created the plate, we captured that magic on wax. Just try to imagine what that would be worth today: the birth of Hip Hop was on a ten-inch record.

Yet, no matter how good the music scene was treating me, and the respect Caz and I earned, we always had to deal with some bullshit discrimination. I remember one afternoon Caz and I were leaving Juanita's house, a girl Caz used to mess with on 182nd and Ryer Avenue. As we were walking out of the building, an older Latino guy started speaking to me in Spanish, asking me what the fuck I was doing, why I was dressed the way I was. "You ain't a real Puerto Rican papa," he said. "Why you trying to be black?"

By this time Caz and I already had a routine for snuffing dudes. Whenever someone crossed the line, Caz would remove my Kangol hat. This time, Caz took off my hat and I took my gun out of my waistband, which scared the shit out of the guy. I told the guy, "Nah, this ain't for you papa," and handed the gun to Caz. When I put my hands up to fight, the guy broke out in to a karate stance. I guess he had been taking lessons, or maybe he had just seen one too many karate flicks in Times Square, because he had the karate stance down pretty good.

I had already been boxing in the Webster PAL for three years and I was a precision puncher. When he came in, I caught his jaw with one of the cleanest punches ever and knocked him unconscious. As Caz handed me my gun back, he stood over the guy and said, "You see you stupid motherfucker. You need to be careful who you talk to like that bro, look at you now. Who's a fake Puerto Rican now?"

Two weeks later Caz and I were standing on the corner of 184th Street talking shit. I had my back to the street and was leaning on a parking meter when all of a sudden Caz's eyes got really huge and he started pushing me out of the way. When I turned to look, the karate kid had tried to stab me with a huge butcher knife, barely missing my shoulder. The Spanish dude thrust the knife with such force that when he missed, he fell into the street and started rolling. I thought about trying to stomp him while he was down but he got up quickly and I had to do something. I reached for my gun only to realize I didn't have the shit with me. So I did the next best thing—I ran my ass off until the guy was nowhere to be seen.

I went looking for the guy a couple of times but never found him. It was good that this guy and I never crossed paths again. If we ever did, he would have been sorry he ever tried to seek retribution. Eventually it became just another funny story about growing up on the streets of the Bronx.

There was a cat named DJ Eddie around our way who wanted to make his name battling Caz and me. We had blown this kid off so many times it wasn't even funny. When it became apparent that he just wasn't going to take no for an answer we decided to throw a jam with him in 183rd Street Park. It was our home court, not that we needed it against this toy, but it was only right to give him a shot to make a name for himself, so we set it up.

July 13, 1977, started out the same as any summer day in the Bronx. We had been in the middle of a ten-day heat wave that made it feel like your skin was going to melt right off your face. The only real fear I had that night was whether or not our small portable fans would keep our amps cool. The amplifiers we used back in those days didn't have internal cooling systems and they got hot even when it was cool outside. I was sure that in that heat we'd be blowing at least one amp if not two, and if Caz and I blew an amp battling this toy ass DJ, I was not going to be happy, and DJ Eddie was going to end up going home with one less amp in his system.

Caz and I had already thrown ten or 15 jams, so when we arrived, we got right to work wiring our shit up by the little parks department house in front of the swings. The house provided a little bit of shade from the brutal sun that was still blaring down on us. DJ Eddie set up on the opposite side of the park and we let him start the jam off. It was about 8:00 PM. There wasn't much of a crowd and there was no reason to start beating this dude this early in the battle. Instead we let him warm up the crowd and practice his shit. And judging from the records he was playing, he was going to need all the warming up he could get.

I got on the set at about 9:00 and started rocking the crowd with some classic funk shit that always made the crowd go crazy. It was a nice night and people were having a good time in spite of the humidity. I felt sticky as shit but I kept doing my thing until around 9:30, when I turned the system over to Caz so he could get busy.

Caz sifted through our crates and threw the first record on the turntable. As he dropped the needle on the record, I heard a normal sound for a few seconds and then I heard *WOOOOOOOOOO WOOOOOOO WOOOOO WOOOOOOOOOOO* as the record slowed to a stop on the turntable.

Shit we lost power!

It wasn't the first time this had happened, but it was too damn hot to be dealing with this bullshit. Just as I was getting ready to check one of the five extension chords we had hooked up, I saw the streetlight above us go *POOF!* The streetlight just blew out. It was quickly followed by a *POOF, POOF, POOF, POOF,* all the way down the block and onto the next block. I watched in amazement as streetlight after streetlight blew out until there were no lights on at all. The Bronx went dark.

I looked back at Caz like, "Oh shit!! Did we just do that? What the fuck did we just do?" I didn't even want to know how much trouble we were going to be in for blowing out every streetlight in the neighborhood.

It was as if I was stuck in a state of shock until being thrust back to reality by a huge *BANG.* When I looked across the street, the bodega owner had just slammed his gate shut, which was soon followed by every other gate in the neighborhood.

BANG, BANG, BANG, BANG!

They were closing their businesses before we could even figure out what had happened. All we knew was that we were illegally jacked up to power and I thought we must have fucked something up on the street and caused the blackout.

The next sign of trouble came when people started screaming, "Hit the stores! Hit the Stores! Hit the stores!" Some fucking idiots took that to mean rob DJ Disco Wiz and DJ Casanova Fly and started running towards us. Before they could get to the ropes we had setup to keep people away from the equipment, Caz and I already had two guns drawn and pointed directly at the crowd.

"Go that way motherfuckers!" Caz demanded while I kept my eye trained on everything moving around us in the darkness of the park. There was no way I would have been able to shoot them all but the first hand that would have passed that rope towards our system would have gotten blown off.

Caz leaned into me and said, "Hold our shit down, Wiz. I'm going to go see if I can get us a new mixer," and with that Caz took off into the night. I began directing my boys in the park to help me pack the shit up real quick. Here we were in the middle of a blackout with every piece of equipment we owned and I was not going to lose one piece of it without shooting someone. Caz returned to the park about fifteen minutes later with one thing and one thing only: a Clubman 2 Mixer. "Yo Wiz, its fucking crazy out here man! Let's get this shit to your house," Caz directed.

After that, Caz and I went our separate ways. I was off to Fordham Road to do some shopping of my own. I first set my sights on the biggest electronics store on Fordham Road, Crazy Eddies. As me and a few of the East Side Boys marched down Fordham Road we got close enough to Crazy Eddies to see shadows on the rooftops. At first I thought the shadows were people trying to break into the store but as we got closer, one of the guys on the roof let off a warning shot into the air. There were about eight guys on the roof, all strapped and ready to shoot the first motherfucker who tried to break into their shop. They were holding their shit down the way Caz and I held ours down a few minutes earlier in the park. So I set my sights on something a little easier to get, and went looking for the nearest sneaker shop, where I filled garbage bags with all flavors of Pumas and Pro-Keds. I had sneakers for years off that shit.

After a while, it got really dangerous being out in the streets. Even though I had a gun with me, there were hundreds of guys with guns out there, so I decided to call it a night after doing my sneaker shopping. I wound up at my girlfriend's sister's house, which was just off Fordham Road. My girl Jeanette was now five months pregnant with our daughter and I spent the rest of the night rubbing her belly and talking to her about how fucking crazy this night had become.

The whole night was surreal. I was running through the streets with people who looked like zombies as they ran in and out of any store that had been compromised. It was as close to complete lawlessness as the city had ever seen and the police were completely outnumbered, in large part due to the fact that 500 police officers had been laid off earlier in the year, and even more were out on leave without pay. Of the police officers that did battle the looters, close to 560 were left injured.

The blackout lasted for 25 hours. When the dust settled and the last fire was put out, the city had been left with $350 million in damage and 4,000 arrests. It was the largest mass arrest in the history of New York City and it forced the city to open jails like the Tombs that had been closed for years, leaving the inmates to be thrown into deplorable rat infested conditions.

Many businesses were put closed for good in one night, and the smartest business owners were the ones who burnt their own stores to the ground in the midst of the chaos. In New York there was no such thing as theft insurance, so firebombing your shop was the only sure way to secure an insurance settlement when all was said and done. Thirty-eight firefighters were injured fighting 851 fires set that night. It was a night of complete anarchy, destruction, and chaos. I fell asleep with my hand on my unborn child wondering what the fuck kind of world I was getting ready to bring her into.

People were starving and they were broke. They saw no opportunities for themselves and they used that night for all that it was worth. When presented with the opportunity to get something for nothing, we took it. These were our reparations for years of living in a nearly bankrupt city that was left by the United States to fend for itself. The shameful irony was the fact that the majority of the lootings were of minority-owned businesses.

Walking the streets of the Bronx the next morning was like walking through a war zone. Even though we were used to seeing burned down buildings for blocks and trash everywhere, what I saw the next morning was beyond comprehension. An eerie calm settled over the neighborhood, while fires still burned and the smell of smoke lingered. A sofa was flipped upside down on a car, alongside with one brand new sneaker, a white t-shirt, and a turkey. Shit was scattered all over Fordham Road for blocks and blocks, and the silence was broken up only by the occasional siren of a fire truck, police car, or ambulance racing to the nearest call. I guess all of the looters had a long night and slept in the next morning.

When the news finally broke and reported that a lightning strike and a poorly trained Con Edison worker were the cause of the worst power outage in the city's history, I had to laugh out loud. Thank God it wasn't Caz and me who caused this mess!

If there is one indisputable fact about the night of the blackout, it would be that a number of DJs sprung up as a result of it. Until that time there were very few DJ crews in the Bronx. The equipment was costly and people didn't really have the means to do what we were doing. Well at least not until the next morning. Out of destruction came new life.

With the explosion of salsa, disco, and punk in New York City during the 70s, it was only natural that Hip Hop would find it's way into the nightclubs. It was only a matter of time before the jams in the parks ended up getting the attention of club owners who needed to bring the next big thing into their clubs to secure their own survival. In 1977 Sal Abbatiello, with the assistance of his father, founded a club called the Disco Fever, originally located at 167th and Jerome Avenue in the Bronx. At first Sal had a white DJ, but he quickly realized Grandmaster Flash would be a much larger draw. When Sal opened the Fever to Grandmaster Flash he not only opened the door to his crowd of followers, he opened the door to Hip Hop. And the Fever would go on to host some of the most legendary performers including Kurtis Blow, Mr. Magic, Grandmaster Flash, and Busy Bee in the early days, and groups like Run DMC, the Beastie Boys, and Heavy D. when Hip Hop went All City.

When the jams moved into clubs, Caz and I kept it going. The Blue Lagoon, located on Webster Avenue and 184th Street, was the first club that Caz and I were able to get down with on a regular basis. It felt good to be in a club doing our thing, but as with anything else in my life there was always some bullshit right around the corner.

This time the owner of the club, an older black guy, decided to play around with our money. First he tried to pay us late and then he tried not to pay us at all. One night I asked him for our money and it turned into a heated argument. I said, "Yo, all I want is our money. You got your money from the door now give us our fucking money, man."

He responded by taking a .25 caliber pistol out of his desk drawer and placing it on his desk.

Oh, this motherfucker thinks he's funny.

I reached into my waistband and showed him that he wasn't the only one in the room with a gun. After a few more heated words he gave us our money, but it shouldn't have gone down like that. After that incident, Caz did all the collecting. I've never understood why people do business like that.

Another club we used to get down at was called Club 462, located on East Third Avenue in the East Tremont section of the Bronx. One night while Caz was doing his thing on the turntables, I noticed that he was really in a zone. He was cutting the records back and forth with so much speed that I grabbed the microphone, which is something I had never really done before. As Caz cut faster and faster, I started to hype the crowd saying, "Faster! Faster! Faster!" and then I threw in "Grandmaster! Grandmaster! Grandmaster!" Just as he had dubbed me DJ Disco Wiz, I returned the favor and named him Grandmaster Casanova Fly, which was eventually shortened to Grandmaster Caz.

One summer night the previous year, Afrika Bambaataa showed up at a jam Caz and I were playing outside at a park called 129, which was off of 180th Street, between Webster Avenue and Southern Boulevard. He just stood there in the back, watching us play, and Caz and I made sure that we played the hottest shit to impress him. I guess it must have worked because he hung around after the jam was over and talked to us about records, sharing his wisdom for what seemed like forever. Bam was always cool with us, like a big brother.

As a member of the Black Spades, Bambaataa had one of the most fearless reputations in the Bronx, and as a major figure in the birth of Hip Hop he was a true testament to the new direction our lives were taking. If any one person could turn the street shit around, stop the madness of the gangs, and bring peace, unity, and love to the Hip Hop movement, it was Afrika Bambaataa. Bam created the mighty Zulu Nation in 1973 and decided to use music, b-boying, graffiti, and MCing as a platform to bridge the gap between blacks and Latinos. In my opinion Bambaataa should have received a Nobel Peace Prize, because nobody else was capable of bringing people together as he did.

At a time when throwing a jam was like playing Russian roulette, Bambaataa parties were know for their peace and unity. Bambaataa and the Zulu Nation were the first to put "Come in Peace" on their flyers and they meant that shit. If you've ever seen the movie *The Warriors* and saw the way Cyrus and the Riffs held down the park, you would know what it was like to go to a Bambaataa joint. The thing is, Bambaataa was doing his thing years before *The Warriors* came out.

Back in those days there were rumors that Kool Herc used to shout out stick-up kids on the mic that were in attendance at his jams. And people even say there were certain records he would play to signal the stick up kids when it was cool to do their thing, to rob people. So Kool Herc jams always had that extra level of danger attached to them. But you just never saw that at Bambaataa jams. When you walked into a Zulu Nation event, Bam's security team, the Zulu Gestapo, was there to hold it down. These cats used to dress with all black fatigues. Most of them were ex-gang members who had been converted into the movement of peace. So it was always cool to go to a Zulu jam.

It was standard practice for DJs to place white labels over their records to cover up what it was they were playing. Kool Herc was infamous for keeping every record he played a secret. But Bambaataa was really open and became a mentor to Caz and I. Being a beat junkie, I always appreciated his willingness to share his knowledge of rare funk beats with me.

Wanting to build our reputation, we told Bam that we'd be honored to have him join us for a battle at the Webster P.A.L., and one night during the summer of 1977 he accepted. It was one thing to show up to our park jam, but to accept a billing with us was only going to take us to the next level. The flyer read Casanova Fly & DJ Disco Wiz featuring Afrika Bambaataa and the Mighty Zulu Nation.

I could feel the energy in the P.A.L. as we prepared for the battle. We offered the only stage to Bambaataa and his crew and we set our system up on the opposite side of the gym. And when Bambaataa played his first few records to warm up the crowd, his system just about blew everybody away.

I still remember the first record Caz put on like it was yesterday. Being the crazy motherfucker that he was, Caz decided to start off the set like this:

We Will, We Will Rock You... Boom, Boom, Cack, Boom Boom, Cack...
We Will, We Will Rock You...

Mr. Biggs who was an MC for the Zulu Nation came on the microphone and screamed out, "CASANOVA, TURN UP YOUR SYSTEM! WE CAN'T HEAR YOU!"

So we cranked our shit up and came back louder:

We Will, We Will Rock You... Boom, Boom, Cack, Boom Boom, Cack...
We Will, We Will Rock You...

Mr. Biggs came back on the microphone even louder this time, "CASANOVA, WE STILL CAN'T HEAR YOU... THIS IS WHAT IT SOUNDS LIKE." And when Bam played the same record on his system, he just about blew us out of the fucking gym...

WE WILL, WE WILL ROCK YOU... BOOM, BOOM, CACK,BOOM, BOOM, CACK...
WE WILL, WE WILL ROCK YOU...

It was funny to us. We packed our shit in and spent the rest of the night with Bam and his crew on stage hanging out, laughing and having a good time. It didn't really matter that we got blown away; the important thing was that we earned the respect of Bam and his crew by having the balls to play with them. A lot of other DJ crews would have never been heard from again, but we came back from it and kept on moving.

After battling Afrika Bambaataa and Kool Herc, Caz and I set our sights on Grandmaster Flash. One night Caz and I went to a Flash jam at the Black Door on Boston Road, where Caz told Flash that we wanted to be on a bill with him at some point in the future. Flash blew us off like we were fucking nobodies. His reply to Caz was, "Nah, nah man," which I immediately took as a sign of disrespect. It's not like we had just landed from fucking Mars. We weren't fucking nobodies in this fucking game, so I got really upset that he was trying to blow us off the way he was.

I got up in Flash's face and started asking him what the deal was. He started to walk away from me so I got even louder and was like, "FUCK Y'ALL MOTH-ERFUCKERS," at which point one of Flash's boys came over to argue with me. We exchanged some words until Caz convinced me to leave it alone and we headed out of the club.

A few days later Caz and I were in the crib making a mixtape and while he was cutting a few break beats up I grabbed the mic and started shouting, "Flash, Flash Kiss My Ass… Flash, Flash Kiss My Ass." It would become a recurring chorus on the next few mixtapes we put out, and it circulated through the Bronx. I'm not sure if Flash ever heard it, but it was just our way of letting him know that we were there.

Track 5: This World Will Rest...

January 12, 1978. The day my daughter Tammy Cedeño was born became the day I fell in love for the first time in my life. Before that moment I never understood when people said they were crying out in joy, but when Tammy was born my eyes immediately filled with tears of happiness. I was a father and I couldn't have been more proud.

Tammy's mother Jeanette was an older girl in my neighborhood who I had been messing around with for a few months. She was a pretty young black girl who came from a good family and she was very sweet. Even though we weren't in a long-term relationship, or even really dating, I wanted to take care of my child and be responsible for the life I was bringing into this world. Although I was only 16 years old I had no issues with being a dad. As a matter of fact, I wanted to make sure I was the best damn father I could be. I had seen the worst a father had to offer and I had no plans of repeating that cycle with my child.

Although I was happy to become a father our families did not feel the same way, and didn't try to hide their feelings. Jeanette and I weren't going to allow that to get in the way and we began making plans to raise the baby together as a family. Throughout the pregnancy I was extremely nurturing towards Jeanette and though she wasn't an overly affectionate person, I was there for her when she needed me. Being in an interracial relationship was hard and we both had to deal with issues of discrimination from our families and our surroundings. I was used to dealing with it being a part of the Hip Hop culture. I already knew what it felt like to have people call me a "nigger lover" way before I started seeing Jeanette, but I knew it was going to be much more difficult for her. It had been years since I dated a Spanish girl and the more involved I became with Hip Hop, the less attractive I became to Spanish girls. All through high school I dated black girls, so it was only natural that Jeanette would now be having my child.

After Tammy was born, Jeanette moved to the Crotona section of the Bronx to live with her family. I'm not sure if her relatives in my neighborhood were trying to get rid of her but I never questioned it. If Crotona was where my daughter was going to be living than that was were I was going to be spending a lot of my time.

The Bronx has always been a very territorial place to live. We very rarely ventured out of our comfort zones unless it was for a jam or to do some dirt, and even then you proceeded with caution and you proceeded with soldiers and artillery. Traveling to the other side of the Bronx presented a new set of day-to-day challenges for me. It was a turbulent time for me, but I was taking on the responsibility of being a father so I made the trek across the Bronx almost everyday of my daughter's life. It was important to me that my daughter understood her father was going to be a strong presence in her life. I never wanted her to feel alone or abandoned, like I sometimes felt. I wanted her to feel wanted, loved, and protected at all times.

Whether I was preparing her Similac milk, changing her diapers, or taking her for long walks to the park with her mother, I loved every second of it. Tammy was growing up fast, and when I blinked a few times my baby was going on six months old. I was enjoying seeing her become more interactive. I would talk to her now and she would talk back in her own form of baby talk. It was one of the most special times in my life and I wouldn't have traded it for the world.

At the same time, a storm was brewing. I discovered that a guy in the neighborhood was turning up the heat on Jeanette every time I wasn't around. He would make advances towards her and if she ignored him he would call her a "stupid bitch" and tell her that he was a real man, unlike that punk he always saw her with. Of course I was the punk he was referring to, and if this motherfucker only knew who I was I'm not so sure he would have been uttering those disrespectful words to her, especially not in the presence of my child. Jeanette knew about my reputation on the streets, she knew I was always strapped, and she knew if I found out what this little motherfucker was doing to my family I'd kill him—so she never told me what was happening.

One night I went with Caz and a few of my other boys including Jeanette's nephew, Skipper, who was a childhood friend of mine, to a Grandmaster Flash jam to see DJ Breakout and Grand Wizzard Theodore at Arthur Park. We couldn't have been there for more than 20 minutes when I heard Skipper say, "Yo Wiz, that's that motherfucker right there."

I had no idea what Skipper was talking about. When I looked closer to see who Skip was pointing at, I immediately recognized him as the dude who seemed to go out of his way to talk to Jeanette whenever I was around. A few times he even ran across the street when I was walking with her to give her a kiss on the cheek and say hello to her. It was as if he was trying to test me, but I just saw him as another knucklehead trying to make himself seem bigger than he really was. Besides, I was usually in daddy mode and that made me more laid back than I might have otherwise been.

Skipper continued, "That's that motherfucker who called Nette a bitch and slapped her in the face because she didn't want him rapping to her anymore."

What the fuck is this dude talking about?

I hope to God this is some kind of misunderstanding because if this dude slapped the mother of my child he wasn't going to be on this earth much longer.

"Yo Wiz, she didn't tell you what happened?"

I grilled Skipper about what had happened and why I was just hearing about it for the first time. "Yo Wiz, we know how you are man. I guess Jeanette didn't want to see you get in trouble over this shit, so she just left it alone."

That was all I needed to know. I walked up to homeboy and asked him, "Yo, you know who I am?"

He replied, "Yeah," with an attitude like I was a little bitch or something.

"You know who my girl is?"

Again, he answered yes. As I started to ask him why he was disrespecting my girl and me, I pulled out the sawed off shotgun I had hidden in my PAL duffle bag.

"Oh man, what the fuck!" He immediately started to cry like a third-grade girl who just had her lunch money snatched by a fifth grader. There were hundreds of people in the park and I was standing in the middle of the crowd with a shotgun pointed right up under this guy's chin ready to leave him fucking headless.

Everyone was frozen, including his crew, and I started screaming on this motherfucker in the park. "If you ever disrespect me or my family, I will fucking kill you where you stand. Do you understand me motherfucker? Do you know who the fuck I am? My name is Disco Wiz. Don't ever disrespect me again or I will kill you."

The dude was begging for his life, apologizing and saying he didn't know as fast as he could. I remember my hand trembling as I held the gun under the guys chin, not because I was scared but because I was two seconds away from committing my first murder. My boys told me to leave homeboy alone, that he was a crying bitch, to put the shotgun away and let him slide. I think they understood that at any moment they could witness someone's head being blown clear off.

As I placed the shotgun in the duffle bag and began walking to a different section of the park, I couldn't help but feel like I had just made one of the biggest mistakes of my life. There was an unwritten rule in the streets that you never pulled out a gun on someone unless you were going to use it, otherwise you would be seen as weak. As I walked away from this guy something in the pit of my stomach told me I would live to regret it.

A few days later I heard through my girl and some of her family that the guy was telling anyone and everyone who would listen that he was going to smoke me.

Shit, if this guy was going to survive in the Bronx he was going to have to do something to get his reputation back. I mean, he had just cried like a little girl in front of hundreds of people in his neighborhood. I understood that he had no choice but to come back at me hard. So now, instead of walking around with one gun I was walking around with two. When I crossed Arthur Park I would pull one of the guns out and walk with it beside me pressed up against my leg. I wasn't taking any chances.

I was upset that things had come to this. I just wanted to be a father. I was trying to stay out of trouble and play that family guy. I was in a bad position, but nobody and I mean nobody in this world had the power to keep me from seeing my little girl. She was one of the only positive things I had in my life.

After a few weeks of walking around on pins and needles I set out to Crotona to take Jeanette for dinner and a movie. I kissed Tammy on the head, cheeks, and neck as she giggled, and told her how much daddy loved her. I was very relaxed, holding my girl's hand while we made our way out onto the street. I had only taken a few steps when I noticed homeboy and a crew of four or five guys trying to surround me on the street. Had they come out blasting they might have caught me off guard but these motherfuckers were trying to push me into a corner. I kept looking for guns as I tried to reach for mine but I couldn't see where any of these dudes were holding anything. No knives, no bats, no guns.

What the fuck was going on?

Someone must have spotted me going into Jeanette's building and had just enough time to rally the troops so that they could exact their revenge. The guy I had beef with started to pop mad shit in my face. "What you gonna do now motherfucker? I got you now motherfucker. What's up now? Now what you gonna do?"

I pulled out my gun and pointed it straight at him and told him to back the fuck up.

"What motherfucker? Fuck you!" he spat.

I guess he didn't believe that I would use the gun. Why should he? I had already pulled out on him and he had lived to see another day. Now I was stuck in a position where it looked like I was all talk and no action, and as he got closer, he tried to snuff me.

BANG!

Oh, shit. What the fuck did I just do?

I saw the look of surprise on his face and as he started to stumble backwards.

BANG!

I shot him again and when he fell to the ground I pointed the gun down on him.

BANG!

BANG!

I shot him two more times. The guys he was with scattered like roaches into the middle of the night.

When I shot him the first time I felt completely threatened. They were closing in on me and I knew that if I didn't do something fast they were going to end up snuffing me, taking the gun, and using it on me. I had no choice, or if I did, I didn't see it at that moment.

I shot him the second time because of the anger that overcame me. This stupid motherfucker just made me shoot him! That might sound crazy but Lord knows I didn't want to do it. I had a daughter, I was a DJ, and things were finally looking good for me in life. The last thing I wanted to do was throw my entire life away because some fucking asshole couldn't take rejection from my girl.

I was so angry that I shot him three more times because I knew he had just cost me my life. He had just cost my daughter her father, a father who wanted nothing more than to correct every mistake his father made when he was raised. After all was said and done this motherfucker had just denied me all my fucking dreams and for that he deserved to die.

When I heard my girl screaming her head off, I snapped back into reality. I was standing there over this dude's lifeless body staring at him knowing I had just killed a man and that I wouldn't be around to raise my little girl. I wanted to cry, but first I wanted to put a few more bullets in this fucking punk.

"Wiz you have to get the fuck out of here!" Jeanette screamed. I saw people staring down on the street. It seemed like every window in the neighborhood went flying open and had someone looking straight down at me. The police were going to have no problems finding witnesses.

Everything was happening in slow motion: I took one last look at the dude I had just shot then started running down Southern Boulevard covered in blood, with a smoking gun in my hand, and no clue of how to escape. I could see the people scattering to get out of my way, ducking behind parked cars, running in buildings, or just laying down on the sidewalk like I was a madman on the loose. Then I got the genius idea to hail a cab, thinking if I could get in a cab and get the fuck out of here I could go to my side of the Bronx where I'd be safe. So there I was trying to hail a cab, still holding the gun, wondering why they wouldn't pick me up. For the first time a real fear set in as I zigzagged between the street and the sidewalk. I heard people screaming and turned around to discover half of the neighborhood chasing me. They were yelling that I had killed their boy and that they were going to kill me. With one bullet left in the gun, I felt the walls closing in around me fast.

I made my way up the steps of the elevated train station on 174th Street and Southern Boulevard, where I hopped the turnstile and ran to the end of the subway platform. It was there that I decided to get rid of the gun, so I leaned down and threw it under the platform. I could see the train far off in the distance, maybe two stations away, but it damn sure wasn't coming fast enough. I paced back and forth for a minute then stood with my back up against the wall, trying to blend in with the other passengers.

Four cops were walking towards me with their guns drawn, followed by some of the guys that had seen the shooting. "Drop the motherfucking gun," the cops ordered, and the guy's friends yelled, "That's the motherfucker who shot our friend! That's him, he killed our boy!"

"Drop the motherfucking gun," they demanded again.

"I don't know what you're talking about. You have the wrong guy. I don't have a gun," I told them.

A few of the cops kept their guns trained on me while another told me to turn the fuck around so that he could handcuff me. As I continued telling them they had the wrong guy, one of the guy's friends came up and punched me in the face after I was already handcuffed. That set off a semi-riot as the rest of the guys who had filled the platform of the subway began trying to attack me while the cops tried to fight them off. Another guy cracked a bottle and smacked me in the face, leaving a scar that remains today.

I respected the way his boys tried to seek vengeance. Had some shit like that happened in my neighborhood, I don't think they could have brought enough cops in to stop us from killing someone who shot one of our boys. So, I respected the way they tried to get to me, but it was real uncomfortable being handcuffed, unable to defend myself.

It took everything the cops had to move me into the little jail cell they had in the subway station, and I could still hear all the commotion outside. I heard so many sirens you would have thought a cop had been shot. When they felt they had enough cops to secure the scene, they rushed me out of the room, down the stairs of the train station, and into an awaiting squad car. It seemed as if hundreds had gathered outside and they were all screaming that they were going to kill me. As the cop car raced off, some of the people started throwing bottles at us. They never stopped trying to get at me and I felt relieved to finally be driving out of that fucking neighborhood.

For the first time I was able to replay the tragic events that had just unfolded. I had killed a man and I was going to jail for life. Tears began racing down my face as I thought about what I had just lost, about what my daughter had just lost. Images of my daughter's first birthday began to play in my head. I wouldn't be there to see her take her first steps, to hear her speak her first words, to witness her first Communion, to dance with her at her sweet sixteen, or walk her down the isle when she got married. It was the first moment I realized what I had just done and what it was going to cost us both. I wanted to give Tammy everything my father failed to give me. I wanted her to be proud of her daddy. I wanted to hold her hand and walk her to her first day of school. I wanted so many things, but as I sat in the back of that police car all I could do was think about the memories I would never be able to make with my little girl. Then I became angry. I had no remorse for what I had just done to that guy because, in my mind, he pushed me to the limit.

When I got to the precinct they put me in the little interrogation room. I had seen this on TV so I just kept my cool. When they asked me over and over why I shot the guy I just kept denying it. I continued to tell them they were confused and that they had the wrong guy. All the while I was hoping they didn't find the gun.

After they took me to Central Booking, they brought me to the hospital and handcuffed me to the bed. I was still bleeding profusely; it took fourteen stitches to close the gash on my face from the bottle attack. As I sat in the hospital bed I began to feel scared about what my actual jail sentence was going to be. I wondered if I would get 25-to-life or if I would get life with no possibility of parole. I thought about how Jeanette would be forced to raise Tammy alone. I thought about my mother, and who would care for her when she got sick again. I thought about my brother and wondered who would protect him now that I wasn't going to be around. I though about Caz and wondered how he would do without me in the battles. I thought about my little girl again but it was too painful. I couldn't have anybody seeing me cry. I was headed to jail for a long time and I was going to have to be cold, be hard, be strong if I had any chance of surviving in there.

When I was released from the hospital, I was brought to central booking, where I learned the guy I had shot was still alive, from a detective, during questioning. I shot him four times, at close range, in the chest and stomach area and was shocked to learn he hadn't died on the spot. For the first time I began to hope that he would live so that my sentence would be lighter. The cops kept telling me to admit that I shot him but I kept quiet. As he began to walk out of the room, he casually said, "Hey I thought you'd like to know we found your gun." The train probably knocked the gun loose as it came roaring into the station and sent it plunging to the street below, where the cops later found it when they canvassed the area.

My bail was $10,000. My mother reached out to her brothers in Miami, but they had long since written me off. When my mother asked if they would assist her in helping to secure a good lawyer the answer was, "Absolutely not!" Instead I was given an overworked and underpaid legal aid lawyer, a very small step above representing yourself. These attorneys could care less about you while they paid their dues, got their experience at your expense, and eventually moved on to better jobs.

After spending two nights in central booking, I was sent to Rikers Island. The small island just off Queens was purchased by New York City from the Ryker family in 1884 and used as a jail farm. In 1932, it was turned into the full-fledged correctional facility now known as Rikers Island. Rikers isn't a long-term prison facility. It is a jail used to process criminals during their court dates. But its history has always been one of violence and torture, and a sentence to Rikers sometimes meant a death sentence no matter what the crime.

I heard a lot of stories about Rikers: the murders, the shankings, the rapes, and the robberies, but I was always good with my hands and had no fear of any man inside. I was going to hold myself down in jail the same way I held myself down in the streets. As I walked through the doors into C-74, one of the most notorious cell blocks in Rikers, I had my game face on. I must have looked crazy walking into jail with my baby blue overlaps and baby blue mock neck shirt completely covered in blood from the shooting and from the bottle being cracked over my face. I had a huge lump on my head and a patch over my eye protecting the fourteen stitches I had received. Even my sneakers had blood on them. When the gates slammed behind me, everything stopped. My life as I knew it was over. I failed my family, I failed myself, and I was about to be paid back for all the dirt I had done on the streets.

I made my way to the recreation room to check out my new surroundings. I watched everyone else in the room doing the exact same thing I was doing: sizing one another up. No one said a word until some asshole decided to test me. "Yo my man, what size are your fucking sneakers?"

I shot back, "Why man, why the fuck you want to know the size of my sneakers?"

"Because I want your fucking sneakers that's why."

'Nah man, you can't have my fucking sneakers unless you can take them from me."

He went off into a corner to wrap his hands in what looked like a thin layer of t-shirt. I took that to mean he wanted to fight so I followed him to his corner and quickly dropped him with two punches.

"Oh shit, my man is nice with his hands," I overheard the Spanish cats in the rec-room saying. It wasn't until much later that I learned there weren't a lot of straight fistfights in jail. Having the boxing background afforded me that level of security that a lot of Latinos didn't have in prison. That's not to say I was the only Latino that was nice with my hands in prison, but I was definitely one of the few. Most Latinos struck fear in the heart of other inmates for being quick to pull out a shank and slice a piece of bread off your fucking ass. I had no problem doing that but it was nice to know that if I got caught without a weapon, I always had a nasty hand game to fall back on.

The first, and only, time Jeanette came to visit me, I saw the look of disappointment and the look of fear in her eyes. As bad as I wanted to breakdown and let her know how sorry I was for abandoning her and the baby, there were no words to express how lost I felt. Although it was tough for me to keep my emotions inside, I was building a reputation as a tough guy and couldn't allow any of the guys to see any kind of weakness inside of me. It killed me that I had lost my daughter and the news Jeanette brought from the outside only made matters worse. She told me the guy I shot still wasn't expected to make it. The bullets had ravaged his body and even if he did survive he would be fucked up for life. I left the visit feeling like I was going to spend the rest of my life in prison, but there was no going back.

I kept my head held high and tried to find some knowledgeable people on the inside who could start educating me about the system. I became close with a Puerto Rican guy who called himself Mathematics. A member of the Five Percent Nation, Mathematics was respected in prison, if not for his massive muscular build, then for his jailhouse intelligence. He played lawyer to a lot of the guys on the Island and also had a very keen knowledge of self. The Five Percent Nation, also know as the Nation of Gods and Earths or the Five-Percent Nation of Islam, was started in the early 60s, in Harlem, after a man named Clarence 13X became excommunicated from the Nation of Islam, adopted the name Allah, and proclaimed himself to be God. The Five Percenter teachings spread into the Bronx and Brooklyn and eventually found its way into the jail system of New York, where many were searching for answers to why they were in the positions of disparity they often found themselves in.

Five Percenters sometimes refer to themselves as scientists and mathematicians who believe in the Supreme Mathematics and Supreme Alphabet, lessons written by Allah. The term "Five Percent" comes from the belief that 85% of the world is easily led in the wrong direction; 10% understand the truth but use it to control the other 85% of the population; and that the remaining "Five Percenters" are the only enlightened beings who possess and use true knowledge to educate the other 85%.

Any positive structure in prison is useful, no matter what the faith based beliefs are. To survive in prison is one thing; to be rehabilitated is another altogether. It's all about being open minded and finding your inner strength, through whatever resources are available to you, to overcome your current circumstances. I never questioned the universe's gifts to me; the Five Percenters' ideology was a necessary step for me on my early quest for knowledge of self.

Mathematics' understanding of the legal system made him someone I needed in my corner at that point in my life. He began schooling me on the best and worst case scenarios. If the guy lived and managed to walk out of the hospital, as a first time violent offender I might walk away with a zip-five, a 0-to-5 year sentence, that would allow me to walk out of jail in two or two-and-a-half years. If he died, I could be hit with a 25-to-life if I was found guilty in trial. As I sat in my jail cell at night waiting to be indicted, I let all of these scenarios run over and over in my head endlessly. The wait was a special kind of torture, which made for never-ending nights on the cellblock.

I'm not sure how long I was at Rikers, but Mathematics told me that if they didn't indict me within a certain window of time, I would be able to walk away free and clear. As it turned out, the guy I had shot wasn't able to identify me through photos and no one else could positively identify me as the shooter. The gun must have been handled by a lot of different people because they couldn't get a clean print off it, and I was beginning to feel like I might walk away from this incident unscathed.

After about six or eight weeks in jail, they transported me to the hospital where the guy was recovering from his wounds, to hold the grand jury hearing. I hoped beyond all hope that the guy would not be able to point me out. As I stood in a makeshift courtroom inside the hospital, I waited anxiously for them to bring this guy into the room in a wheelchair. When the doors swung open, I saw them wheeling an entire hospital bed into the room. The guy was hooked up to all kinds of machines. As the bed came to a rest a few feet away from me, I looked over. I was shocked and repulsed by what I saw.

His chest and stomach looked like a subway map of the city with the hundreds of stitches like endless lines of train tracks. It was sickening to see what I had done to him and it was the first time I felt bad for him. I was horrified by what I had done to him, and my heart sank deeply for the obvious pain I had brought into his life. Those feelings of sorrow were soon overshadowed by my feelings of failure; when they asked him if he recognized the person who shot him and he pointed to me. I knew I was fucked.

Both the guy and I were victims of our environments. At the time, neither of us seemed to have a choice in the matter, and we both suffered in the end. I saw him once later, in 1983, while I was visiting some of my friends on Crotona Avenue; Skipper pointed him out as he crossed the street and walked past me in a drugged-out haze. It was eerie. I looked right into his eyes as we passed each other on the very same sidewalk where I had shot him five years earlier. He didn't recognize me. It seemed like a million years had passed between us. I would later learn that he had died of AIDS-related complications in the mid-90s.

While going to trial for the shooting, I spent nearly a year on Rikers Island while the biggest idiot the Legal Aid Society had ever placed on its payroll handled my case. The only thing this young, uneducated, incompetent, male attorney had to offer was a plea bargain agreement. The system is so fucked up that you can literally cop a 7-to-15 year plea on triple homicide or face 25-to-life three times over if you go to trial and are found guilty. The system is built to get you in and out. Fuck justice. Fuck the truth. If you don't have the money to hire a high-powered attorney, you are going to jail for a long time.

I had so many charges on me that I don't think my lawyer knew what half of them were. He didn't care that I was defending myself from a guy threatening to kill me and it didn't matter that this guy had already assaulted my girlfriend. I was being offered plea deals of 12-to-15 years, which were higher than what some guys were offered for murder. I wasn't taking any fucking plea deal. I was going to fight this out and go to trial for attempted murder in the first degree. My only hope was that the jury would have some understanding of what we face in the hood, but destiny had other plans for me. On the eve of jury selection, my lawyer came to see me with a last minute plea deal. He told me the state was now offering a 0-to-9 year sentence, which meant I could do up to nine years in jail. "Luis, if we don't take this deal you could spend 25 years in jail," my lawyer said. I took the deal. I wanted to be free before I turned 40 years old, and to see my daughter before she turned 21.

I'll never forget the day I walked into court to cop that plea. It was a dehumanizing experience. The judge asked me to repeat my name and to agree that I was guilty of attempted murder in the first degree, assault in the first degree, and assault with a deadly weapon. It seemed like the process went on forever and it made me almost too weak to stand. I felt like an animal standing up there, being judged and admitting to the world that I was guilty of such a heinous crime, without being able to explain my side. I wish I were given the opportunity to say, "I only wanted to see my daughter grow up."

When I went back to my cell that night, I cried like I had never cried before in my life. I punched the walls and destroyed everything in my cell. I let out all the emotion that had been building up inside of me since my arrest. In my rage I barely heard a voice scream out, "It's OK Wiz. It's going to be all right, man!"

The guys on my cellblock told me it was okay to release that shit, they told me it happened to all of us. I was 17 years old and I had just been sentenced to nine years in prison. As my bus headed upstate I envisioned the streets at rest. It would be years before they would hear from the likes of DJ Disco Wiz again. My family, my friends, my music career, and most of all, my daughter, were gone. My life was over and anybody in Elmira Correctional Facility who got in my way was going to wish they were never fucking born.

Track 6: Peace Will Come...

I heard a lot of stories about Elmira. Everybody told me, "When you get upstate it's gonna be a different story, son," but I reminded myself that the same stories I had heard about the Island never happened to me. I would never allow myself to become a victim. After a year on Rikers I had put on fifty pounds of pure muscle. When I first went into jail I was a skinny little dude, but I spent a lot of my time doing what everyone else was doing, hitting the weights hard, doing push ups and pull ups in my cell, and using my bed as my own weight machine. Now when I hit dudes in their face, I broke bones. I would never let another man disrespect me in any way, and I would die before I let another man make me his bitch. My world had already been destroyed and as far as I was concerned, I had nothing left to live for.

On the eight-hour bus trip to Elmira I was numb but not scared. There's definitely a difference. Some cats were quivering right through their clothing. I felt bad for them, they'd be someone's bitch the second they stepped off the bus, but I didn't spend too much time worrying about them. Instead I was looking out at the countryside, a beautiful and bittersweet ride upstate. It would be a long time before I would see freedom again.

Elmira was a processing location for inmates. Once you arrived, the prison officials would determine where you'd spend the remainder of your bid. For some inmates Elmira became their final home while others were scattered throughout the upstate prison systems of Clinton, Greenhaven, Woodhaven, or Coxsackie to name a few. If there was one thing the state of New York didn't lack, it was prisons.

Going to Rikers was nothing like walking into Elmira, where I was being stripped down with hundreds of other inmates and told, "Lift your ball sack, stick out your tongue, and say 'ahh,' motherfuckers. Now bend over, spread your fucking ass cheeks, and cough." After that we were sprayed for lice like a herd of animals. When the processing was complete, we took our bags and walked down a long hallway past hundreds of older inmates talking about who was going be their bitch. The shit talking went on all night long but the second day, all the shit talking stopped and no one said a fucking word to our faces.

I never had a chance to settle in Elmira. After spending a week there, I was shipped to Coxsackie Correctional Facility to do my bid. Coxsackie was a Maximum-A prison and housed some of the most hardened criminals the state had ever seen. The prison was packed with tough guys and almost all of them were under 30—from the fellas doing five-year bids for violent acts, to the 17-year-old lifers who would never see the light of day. You can't punish a man who's already lost his life—it's just not possible—and it made Maximum-A prisons a deadly place to dwell.

New inmates have to be on the lookout for the bootie bandits (homo thugs) who prey on the young and weak, and lure them with free gifts from the commissary and protection from other inmates, in exchange for sexual favors. These guys are known as Maytags because they have to wash the other man's clothing and serve as an inside bitch. Then there are the punks who manage to fight off the bootie bandits but are too soft to survive. If they don't end up in PC (protective custody), another inmate will extort them for protection money and make them a son; the cost for protection is everything, from money, clothes, cigarettes, and soap, to cookies, jewelry, and even naked pictures of their girlfriends.

The day I arrived at Coxsackie I was walking through the mess hall when I heard a voice break through the thickness of the noise, "Yo Lou!"

When I turned around I recognized my boy Frankie Lee from the old neighborhood. All I could say was, "Oh shit!"

Frankie had murdered a guy named Manny, right in front of my building, a few years earlier. Manny was a huge, muscle-bound monster whose mere presence was intimidating as hell. When Frankie found out Manny was messing around with his girl he decided to shoot him with his .25. Why get into a fistfight with someone twice your size when you can just blast him and call it a day? Frankie ended up with a 25-to-life bid.

Who knew Coxsackie was going to be like a reunion for me? I ran into another one of my boys, Toby, who was doing a seven-and-a-half-year bid for armed robbery. I had only been in Coxsackie for a matter of hours and it felt real good to know I wasn't standing alone in this place. I wouldn't have to go through the process of providing my resume to the jailhouse population; my boys would spread the word about who I was, and what I was about. I was able to walk around jail no different than if I was on the streets. Although the rough reality of being locked up with a bunch of animals never tested me, the racial segregation in prison made me understand that shit was serious in prison. The inmates divided themselves along racial lines, and I had trouble dealing with that because I didn't like being told who I could and couldn't hang out with. I was my own man and I never let that shit fly on the streets. I wasn't about to start now.

Frankie introduced me to his crew and let me know he was running shit in there. The crew was all Latinos, the same Spanish cats that despised me out on the streets for the way I dressed, being involved with Hip Hop music, and dating black girls, but Frankie was my man so I was going to run with his crew and feel things out. As time went on people in the crew began to respect me. My Hip Hop involvement became kind of a novelty to them, but some of the more uptight Latinos tried to tell me that I should leave that shit alone. They took every opportunity to say, "I wish you wouldn't talk like a *cocolo* and hang out with *cocolos. Oye tú eres Puertorriqueño, todo esa gente son para ellos.*" They were telling me that I should only be for Latinos because black people were only for themselves. They told me, "Leave that fucking jungle music alone."

I told them I couldn't do that. I wasn't in there to pick sides or to have my life dictated to me. I respected their choices and expected to get that same level of respect in return. Then one day Frankie told me, "Yo Lou, I just gotta tell you, man. If shit gets crazy in here I can't back you up."

"Frankie, you do what you gotta do, bro. I'm gonna be me regardless."

With that, the conversation about race ended. I knew it was merely a game of survival and numbers. We had to stick together to survive and the brothers felt the same way. Soon enough the conversations changed from the color black to the color green. We'd sell anything we could get our hands on, from cigarettes to snacks to protection. I was seen as an enforcer and made sure no one got hurt on my watch. As time went on, more fellas from the neighborhood came upstate and we'd immediately bring them into the family, providing them with protection and brotherhood. We'd always look after our own. In that regard it was a blessing to be from a fucked up neighborhood.

I wasn't only running with guys from my old neighborhood; I was also meeting brothers from other boroughs like Brooklyn and learning from them. Brooklyn was infamous for its stick-up kids and being in jail with them taught me everything I needed to know about the stick-up game. I considered Brooklyn dudes as real as they fucking came and I respected the pride they carried around for their homes with slogans like, "Bed Stuy: Do or Die," and "Brownsville: Never Ran, Never Will." I had a great deal of respect for their take-no-shit attitudes and brave heart ways.

A few months after arriving at Coxsackie I got to see the results of politics and pay coming into play in the prison system. One morning in 1979, all the prison guards just walked off the job after the negotiations for a new contract fell apart. New York Governor Hugh L. Carey had no choice but to call in the support of the National Guard. The strike lasted 17 days and it was an uncomfortable time for everyone. The guys in the National Guard didn't know how to treat us humanely and we went a full week without being able to shower. The prisoners took to throwing garbage and toilet paper at the guards and we'd hang sheets out the cellblock windows to alert the passing media helicopters with messages like, "HELP! These motherfuckers aren't treating us right. They won't even let us shower. HELP US."

We couldn't always see what was going on outside the prison, but we heard the fights between the corrections officers and the National Guardsmen who had to cross the picket lines to enter the prison, and wondered if any of the guards would end up in jail like us.

The conditions were horrendous and by the time the real prison guards returned we were actually happy to see them back. At least they knew how to keep the assembly line of prisoners fed and bathed, and that was humanity at its most basic level. Seventeen days seemed like a year and a half, and it felt good to get back to our normal routines after all that madness.

Once things calmed down after the strike, jail really started to become my home. The only outside contact I had with the world was the perfume-laced letters and half-naked pictures from Jeanette but eventually she too would disappear. In one letter she told me she was dating a younger cat named Melvin from 183rd Street. What a fucking insult. The least the bitch could have done was go up to 196th Street to find a new dude.

When you go to jail you are dead to everyone on the outside world except your mother. You have no crew, no family, no girlfriend, and no kids. Only the woman who birthed you has the patience, love, and understanding to stand by you. Everyone else pretty much forgets you ever walked the earth. Honestly, if I had my way, my mother never would have come up to see me at all. I hate the fact that she made those eight-hour trips in her condition; it shamed me deeply. I was truly happy to see her, but always asked her not to return; I told her I was doing okay. She never listened. A mother will always be a mother no matter what. She stood by me all those years while everyone else wrote me off and turned their backs on me—like Jeanette.

I never expected Jeanette to be faithful to me while I was locked up. I learned pretty fast that there were two worlds, the one in which I was doing my bid, and the one outside that we all used to call the "real world." I never got them confused—ever! I shut myself out for many years and this mindset helped me keep my sanity. I never thought for a split second that Jeanette or any other woman would stay true to her man while he was locked up—that would just be stupid thinking.

Still, Jeanette had a real gift for picking men; a few years later I saw Melvin up in Coxsackie and could literally smell his fear. Melvin was from a group of younger cats in my neighborhood who looked up to me—but that didn't stop him from fucking my girlfriend while I was locked up; I guess he never thought he would find himself on the inside with me. A lot of people feared me when I was out on the streets and these same people were filling his head with bullshit, that I was going to hurt him if I ever saw him again. He tried to apologize to me and said he didn't know how he even ended up dating her. I didn't feel the need to exploit him any further; I just laughed, gave him a hug, and said, "I hope you enjoyed the pussy because its gonna be a minute before you get that shit again." He was far from Valentine Avenue, in a very scary place, and I wanted him to know he was my little homeboy no matter what, and that I would always have his back at Coxsackie.

Every once in a while I'd receive a letter from Caz. He'd run into mutual friends we had who'd been released and they'd tell him how I was doing. Little did I know that while I was making a name for myself in prison, Caz was on the streets making a name for himself in the Hip Hop history books.

The first time I heard Caz on the radio I was in my cell listening to a local Albany station. When I heard, "I'm the C-A-S and the O-V-A, and the rest is F-L-Y," I almost hit the fucking ceiling. I knew those lyrics from all of our routines in the parks and at the clubs. I was like, "Damn, that's my man on the radio! He's done it. He's blowing up!"

Although it was the first time I got respect, praise, and understanding from my Latino brothers for being involved in what they saw as a purely black movement, they didn't give a fuck about Hip Hop in general. It was the late 70s/early 80s and it was too early for them to grasp the movement's impact. Instead I mostly talked about Hip Hop with the black population, who had a deeper sense of knowledge and appreciation for the culture. And my relationship to Hip Hop gave me a new level of celebrity status behind bars. The entire jailhouse was in love with the fact that our music, the music from the streets, was on the radio, and it was only the beginning of things to come.

At the same time, hearing Hip Hop music over the radio was a bittersweet moment; I felt like both a success and a failure. I was locked up and missing out on the opportunity to be involved with some groundbreaking shit, something we had started together. But feeling sorry for myself only lasted seconds. I was mad proud of Caz and I called him to congratulate him on his success.

"Yo Caz, what the fuck! I heard you on the radio kid, you're blowing up!" I screamed into the phone.

"Nah Lou, that's not me."

"What the fuck you mean that's not you? Those are your lyrics, bro. I heard you on the radio."

I couldn't believe Caz was trying act like he wasn't on the radio, until he told me that some other nigga was using his lyrics. "Yo Lou, it's me but it isn't really me, you know what I'm saying."

I was shocked and couldn't comprehend how someone else was rocking on the radio with my man's lyrics but I respected the fact that he really didn't want to get into details, so we cut the call short.

I later found out that Sylvia Robinson, who founded Sugar Hill Records, happened to hear Big Bank Hank (Henry Jackson) rapping along to a Caz tape in the pizza shop where he worked. She asked Hank to become a member of the Sugar Hill Gang and he went on to use Caz's lyrics in "Rapper's Delight," the first Hip Hop record to make the Top 40 charts. "Rapper's Delight" would go on to become the biggest Hip Hop record of all time and became synonymous in the public's mind with the birth of Hip Hop music. Caz never received any credit or financial compensation for his lyrics, and to this day when I hear Hank spit those lyrics, I feel sick to my stomach.

When I learned the truth about "Rapper's Delight," I understood what my arrest had cost him. Had I been in the streets at that time I would have made damn sure Hank would have provided some form of credit and compensation to Caz. Don't get me wrong—I'm not saying that Caz couldn't take care of himself; I'm just saying that we had each other's back to the extreme. We were brothers and I felt bad that I wasn't there for him when he needed me most.

But my reality was jail and it was ugly. I never got used to the way the guards treated us. Everything they did, from the way they looked at you to the way they talked to you, made you feel like you were less than a man. Prison was like the worst military school times 10, and I often found myself hit with citation after citation for breaking their rules. It doesn't matter how tough you think you are; at the end of the day you have to learn responsibility and to abide by their set of rules. Sure the prisoners had their own codes of conduct and their own sets of rules, but all those rules went out the window when it came time to answer to the damn guards.

For me, a man with a lot of pride who didn't allow my father to tell me what to do, learning to take orders from a bunch of white boys with sticks was one of the hardest lessons I've ever had to learn. They'd literally tell you when to eat, sleep, shit, and shower. They'd tell you when to line up, when to stand, and when to sit. It was completely dehumanizing. It's designed to humiliate you and break you down to nothing. It always bothered me that they had no idea what we went through on a daily basis. After having such a violent past, being humiliated and talked down to was the last thing I wanted to deal with on a daily basis. Every time a guard got out of line with me I felt like I was looking in the eyes of my father and I wanted nothing more than to pound them into the ground, to look down on their bleeding body and say, "What now motherfucker?"

At any time, these guards could tell you to drop your pants, bend over, and spread your cheeks. They'd tell you to turn around and lift your nut sack. It was like they got a sick pleasure out of torturing us, raping us mentally, and laughing about it later. I don't think any man should ever be subject to this kind of mental cruelty but once you land in prison, you are treated as less than human and you have no rights. It's a good fucking reason not to land in jail in the first place.

With my blood boiling over the treatment I was receiving from the prison guards, it was only a matter of time before I would explode. One day while lining up a group of prisoners, a guard walked over to me and yelled in my face, "Get in the line, boy!"

I took a step back into line and threw everything I had into the knockout punch. He never had a chance to react. I could hear prisoners yelling, "Oh shit," as he went crumbling down to the ground. The last thing I saw was blood gushing from his face as fellow guards came to his rescue. I didn't put up a fight, and allowed them to drag me to a room off the hallway where one guard after another jumped on me until they covered every inch of my body, which was now wrapped up in a fetal position on the floor in an attempt to block the most devastating blows to my head and face. I could feel them beating every inch of my body from my back to my balls. They were using everything they had, from their fists and feet to their sticks and elbows. Then I was handcuffed and stripped naked unable to protect any part of my body as the beating intensified. The thing that stands out most in my mind was the boots that were kicked up my ass as far as possible. *Fuck, I'll have to think twice about punching out a guard next time.* It was another way to completely degrade us; for weeks after my face and body healed, I still had trouble shitting and pissing.

But more than the physical pain were the words they threw at me while doling out their form of justice: "This ain't New York motherfucker. We're gonna kill you up in here," and, "You'll never see the light of day you fucking spic. You ain't gonna live through this."

Although I couldn't fight back physically, I don't believe I ever made much of a sound. I saw no reason to give them the satisfaction of seeing me in pain, and it probably made them beat me longer and harder. I must have become unconscious at some point because when I finally came to, I was in the bing, a holding cell where they took violent perpetrators. I was butt naked and bleeding from every orifice of my body, and once they realized I was conscious, they beat me until I was knocked out a second time.

I can't say I regretted it, punching that guard. It felt good, if only for a second in time, to take control of my life, my emotions, and my manhood. It felt good to take back control of my destiny no matter how fucked up that destiny became the moment I laid that guard out. I was in control again.

For my offense, in addition to the physical punishment, I landed myself in the hole for thirty days. It's not a good place to be when you're trying to heal from massive bodily injuries but it does toughen you up. By the time I came out I was a legend within my crew. My beard was down to my neck. My body was still fucked up physically, but mentally I was tougher than ever. They didn't break me.

It wouldn't be until later that the true punishment for my actions would be felt, that being when I saw the parole board for the first time at Elmira in February 1979, when I first went upstate to be processed. I knew the first visit was just a formality and I never expected to be released. I just showed up and listened to the parole board hit me with another eighteen months. With time already served that meant I would see the parole board again six months after arriving at Coxsackie. I knew there was no chance they'd be cutting me loose, so I went into the meeting like a zombie, listened to them talk about what a danger I was to society, and went back to my cell with another year to serve before I'd be eligible for parole.

After serving a total of two-and-a-half years in prison I began to believe I might have a shot at being released at my third board visit. I'm not sure why I felt like this; it's not like I was a model prisoner in any form. I was doing all the wrong things. I was running with a bunch of lifers like Frankie Lee. It was the lifers who would never see the light of day no matter what they did or how they acted behind bars. They'd never go home unless it was in a box.

As I prepared to see the parole board for the third time, I realized I had no idea what I had to do to gain my freedom. I saw people leave prison all the time and even though I was happy for them it would tear me apart to know I wasn't the one going home. I'd watch the prison buses pull out and see my friends waving good-bye. Before they left, the freshly paroled convicts would give away all their prison possessions to their brothers. They'd bless us with their books, their clothing, and any snacks from the commissary. It was the last good a prisoner could do before leaving you behind for the fresh air of freedom.

I learned a lot about brotherly love in prison. On the streets most of the friendships were superficial but in prison you bonded with people on a level most only experienced in battle. You had to see these guys everyday whether you were in a good mood, bad mood, felt like joking or felt like fighting. We were all locked in the same big cage together and stuck with each other through the good, the bad, and the ugly. We became each other's therapists. I'd talk about my ex-girlfriend and how much I missed her or how she did me wrong, and then another brother would open up about his ex-girlfriend and how he was done wrong. We became a tight support system for one another and I learned the importance of trusting my emotions with those around me, a lesson I never would've learned on the streets of the Bronx.

A lot of the talk was of a sexual nature. We'd talk about what we'd done sexually to our girls on the outside world and come back from visits talking about each other's mothers. "Son, I saw your moms in the visiting room and she is fine as fuck man. I bet your mother has a nice pussy." I'm not sure that would have flown in the outside world, but that is the kind of camaraderie we had on the inside. Nothing was off limits. Shit, we had no place to go so we had to talk about everything and anything, and learn to laugh about it. It was in prison that I finally learned how to snap on dudes. I was always wound tight on the streets and I didn't take jokes lightly, but inside I learned how to make fun of my brothers and make fun of myself. It was an important lesson on humility, and I learned how to be comfortable with who I was.

There were no pussies in my circle. It wasn't like being in the streets, where people knew of your reputation and steered clear of you because they knew you packed heat or were good with your hands. Inside you had to be tough, because all you had were your hands, and even if you were lucky enough to have a shank, you still had to get up close enough to stab him. So it was just a different level of gangster. In jail I didn't have the edge with my hands. No matter how nice I was with my boxing game, there was always someone just as nice. So I always proceeded with admiration for the other tough guys I was surrounded by and they maintained the same respect for me.

The week leading up to my third parole board visit, I didn't really know how to feel or what to think. I wasn't yet being mentored about ways to get out of prison.

I had done nothing to warrant these people sending me home early. They considered me one of the knuckleheads, beyond rehabilitation. And the sad thing is that they weren't far off the mark. If they thought I was bad when I went into prison, they had no idea that I considered myself much worse now—because once you get over that initial fear of going to jail there is very little that will stop you from going back.

I sat down in front of the parole board looking at people who looked nothing like the people in my neighborhood, nothing like me. These people didn't represent me. They didn't know my struggle and I'm sure they didn't care. I sat at that table with nothing in front of me. I'd done nothing while in prison to prove I'd be able to become a productive member of society once released. No schooling, no programs, nothing but citations for bad behavior.

The first question was, "Mr. Cedeño, do you have anything positive to report to the board?"

Report? Shit, I didn't prepare any report.

I guess he could tell I had a confused look on my face and nothing to offer, so he jumped right into the next question. "Do you feel any remorse for your crime Mr. Cedeño?"

Why the fuck does this guy keep calling me Mr. Cedeño? My name is Lou, motherfucker. At least that's what I was thinking before I gave him the standard answer I had practiced in my cell. "Yes sir. I feel a lot of remorse for my crime, a lot. I have since the moment I committed the crime."

Should I say a lot again?

"Do you believe you've been rehabilitated?"

"Oh yeah, yeah, no doubt. I'm good. I'm ready to go home."

"Mr. Cedeño what I'm asking is why do you feel we should let you go home? Do you feel you can be a productive member of society again? Do you feel like you can be functional on the outside world? Do you have anything to offer the outside world when you are released from prison?"

Dude, I just want to go the hell home so I can be with some bitches and get back to the block and see what's going on out there in the real world. Do I have something to offer the outside world? Yeah my dick, motherfucker.

What was I supposed to say to this man? I haven't become a scientist or a doctor in here. I've honed my criminal instincts. Does he want to know that?

I wasn't even listening to him any longer. Instead I was rehearsing the lines my homeboys inside had taught me about being fully rehabilitated. Then he asked one more time, "Mr. Cedeño, why should we release you?"

I wasn't able to tell these people about all the pain I felt when I lost my six-month-old baby girl. I wish I could have told them how badly I wanted to go home and be a good father to my daughter, be a good son to my mother, to become the man I desperately wanted to be. Instead all I could say was, "I want to go home."

"Mr. Cedeño, the board doesn't feel you're ready to be released back into the world. Your request for parole is denied. We'll see you again in 24 months. Do yourself a favor and work harder on your rehabilitation."

I remember at that very moment staring off into space as if I had just been sentenced for the first time. I might not have believed I was going home walking into that room, but something funny happens when you sit in front of the board. You begin to convince yourself that maybe there is a chance you'll be released after all. Maybe they'll see something in you that will give them compassion for your situation. Maybe you'll remind one of them of their son, cousin, or brother. Maybe they'll find a way to see through to the heart you've buried for so long.

As I walked back to my cell I could feel myself getting angry at the assholes I was surrounding myself with in jail. I had all these fucking jailhouse lawyers preaching to me about how I was a first time offender. They'd say, "Yo, you always go home on your third board. You're as good as free," and I believed them. I even had the lifers telling me they had dibs on my shit, "Yo son, you don't need those kicks anymore, you a free man." Another would say, "Yo Wiz, I want those pants before you go home."

To be walking back to my cell now, devastated me to the core of my being. I wondered how the fuck everyone could be so wrong. My anger began to boil over to the point that I had to transfer this shit out of my body and into someone else's. I felt the beef coming as I walked out to the yard with the piece of paper in my back pocket that read, "DENIED."

I wondered who was stupid enough to send an angry inmate who had just been denied his freedom back into the yard. These fucking knuckleheads running the system probably waited to see the beef unravel. They had to know that an angry convict walking out into general population could only mean problems, but I guess they got a kick out of seeing a bunch of animals chew on one another.

I stood there in a daze of confusion wondering what I'd do next. I was thinking about when I'd ever get the opportunity to actually go home, when a handball hit me on my arm. A voice broke my thoughts and asked, "Yo, can I get the ball?"

When I looked up, I saw this bushy haired bastard from Brooklyn. I recognized him as an ex-gang member they called Blood.

"Yo, yo my man, can I get the ball," he demanded. On any other day this would've been nothing more than a fair request, but this wasn't any other day. This was the day I just found out my ass was staying in jail for another two years.

"Yo my man, get your own fucking ball," I shouted back.

Blood came walking up to me but he never had the chance to say another word. As soon as he got within striking distance I punched the shit out of him. When all was said and done he had blood coming out of his mouth, a few missing teeth, and a dazed fucking look on his face. I hit him so hard one of his teeth broke the skin of my left hand and left a scar that remains today. Before I could think twice about what I had done I was once again covered in guards being dragged off to the hole.

Fuck it, the hole was the place I needed to be, alone with my thoughts and pain. I didn't need to be released back to my cell right then because I might have had a few words to say to the jailhouse lawyers that had mistakenly given me the worst kind of gift you could ever give an inmate—false hope.

When I was released from the hole the next day I had to watch my back because Blood ran with a crew of bushy haired ex-gang bangers and he'd most likely feel the need to retaliate. When I ran into him several days later, I figured homeboy was coming over to shank me but he kept it real, "Yo dude, I respect whatever happened man. I ain't got no beef with you." I told him why I had reacted the way I did and he sympathized with me. *He fucking sympathized with me after what I had done to him.*

Over the next few years Blood and I became pretty good friends. It was a humbling experience for me to learn that a man could swallow his pride and build a friendship with someone who had disrespected him in prison. Blood wasn't a punk, but I guess he had a deeper understanding of what it was that had placed us all there in the first place. It was a lesson I'd have to learn if I ever hoped to go home. I was going to have to make peace with my past and with my present before I'd ever be able to see a future.

Track 7: Don't Know What... We're Running From

His name was Peace. He was serving out several life sentences for murder and would never see the light of day again as a free man. Respected and feared, Peace didn't talk to anyone outside of his immediate circle. He was a real cold motherfucker. At the time I believed Peace didn't speak to me because I rolled with *morenos,* and to me he was a nobody, until a chance encounter taught me different.

A few days after being released from the hole for punching out Blood, Peace stepped to me and said, "Yo, I want to talk to you."

"Yeah what's up," I shot back.

"I know who you are and I want to tell you a couple of things. I know everything about you man. I know who you are on the street. I know about your reputation. I know who you are in here. And I want you to know that you ain't shit man. You ain't nothing. You ain't doing nothing with yourself, and you ain't half of the man you think you are."

Who the fuck was this guy to be telling me about myself?

I guess he could see the anger beginning to build on my face, and he quickly went from telling me who I wasn't to telling me who he was. "I killed three people man. I was hit with multiple life sentences. I'm gonna be in this fucking place for the rest of my life. How do you think I feel about that? You think I don't have children in the street? Yo, do me a favor and look at me when I talk to you man. I'm gonna be here my whole life. You think I don't have family out on the street, a girl I left behind? You think I don't have a mother? I will never see them again as a free man. I'll never see the streets again."

The words coming out of Peace's mouth were real and raw. He spoke with conviction and honesty and he definitely had my undivided attention.

"You stupid man," he said. "I don't care if you get offended but I have to tell you. You're being real fucking stupid. I know that you ain't doing nothing to change your life for the better. I got my education in here. I'm working towards a second degree. I've been here a long time but it's still important to me to keep my mind awake, so I can help other brothers who want to be helped. Do you want to be helped brother?"

All I could do was shake my head and listen intently to the words he was speaking. "I'm gonna die in here. Do you understand what I'm trying to tell you bro? I'm gonna *die* in here."

All I could say was, "Yeah."

Peace asked me if I cared about my family, and when I answered with an un-questionable yes, he told me that I had to prove that I cared with my actions not just my words. He told me up to that point in time, I wasn't doing that. What I was doing was proving to the world that I wasn't worth rehabilitation and that I wasn't worth being released back into society. "Show the world that you care. Stop fucking conforming to what the system believes you to be; an animal, less than a man, less than a human being."

No one had ever spoken to me like that and walked away with a mouth full of teeth. Most people would have been afraid to speak to me that way, but Peace had nothing to fear. I guess the only way he could ever truly feel alive was to use his power to help brothers like me. We spoke for hours about what made a man smart as opposed to ignorant. He broke things down to me that I never thought about and he told me how to use the system while I was a part of it, to become educated, to become stronger. "Your hands don't make you a man. Your hands don't make you strong. It's what's inside your head that makes you tough. You have to fight with your knowledge, and you can gain knowledge of self by educating yourself. Lou, don't you see, an education can never be taken from a man. You can take his house, his car, his money and even his job; shit, you can definitely take his woman, but you can never take his intelligence."

I was a little embarrassed when he asked me if I had a high school diploma. When I told him I didn't, he explained to me that my first step should be going to school. At the same time he said I needed to get a job and learn a trade. "If you keep running around here with these fucking knuckleheads that's all you're ever gonna be. And I see you running around with all these *morenos*, I don't know about that either."

"Yo I grew up around *morenos* my whole life and I've never had a problem with them, that's a part of who I am," I shot back.

"I'm not judging you man. I just want to tell you that the next time you see an-other board, if you don't take nothing to them, you're gonna do the whole fucking nine years. You will do everyday of those nine years. *Tú sabes, eso es lo que tú quieres, eso es lo que te va a pasar.*" If that's what you want, that's what you'll get. Peace was warning me that if I kept walking the path I was on, the next time I punched some-one in the face, they might decide to end my life right there on the spot.

Peace reached me in a way I don't think many would have been able to. It had to be someone I respected, someone who I felt had walked a similar walk and lived a similar life. I respected the wisdom Peace had and the knowledge he gained through his years of hard living, pain, and struggle. I was awake now, and I had no intention of going back to sleep.

A few days later I was enrolled in pre-GED classes. Going to school at night kept me focused, kept me out of trouble, and set me on the path towards becoming an educated Latino. When I hit the streets I wasn't going be the same ignorant person. I was also receiving an education in what it meant to be a Latino man. I didn't know how hard our people had worked to be able to gain a position in this country. I didn't know about the history of my people who were conquered and enslaved by the Spaniards and other Europeans.

The Christopher Columbus I learned about in school was a great explorer, whose voyages led to the discovery of many far off worlds including the Americas, Cuba, and Puerto Rico. But we are celebrating a man who never really discovered anything; Columbus merely landed in parts of the world already inhabited by the likes of the Lucayan, Taino, and Arawak people, indigenous to the Caribbean. Yet they were treated as unfit to inhabit their own land; they were, pillaged, murdered, or enslaved. According to a log transcribed by one of Columbus' associates on his voyage to the Americas, he felt he had the power and the right to conquer and govern the people of the islands. He even refused to allow the people of Hispaniola to be baptized since Christians could not be slaves.

How come I never read about this Columbus in school?

Reading about what the people of Puerto Rico and Cuba went through in the past made my troubles in the South Bronx seem a little less gruesome, but no less important. It was part of the same vicious cycle passed down from generation to generation.

I knew so little about the history of my people. Yeah, I knew the language and I knew what we ate. I knew that my people were from Cuba and Puerto Rico, but I didn't understand why Americans called me a spic and looked down on me. As I read more, it began to make sense. They'd discovered us as free men, enslaved us, and expected us to serve them for all of history.

It took a Dominican brother named Peace to educate me and introduce me to my ancestry, to help me understand why we were such proud people and why we were so passionate about life. Once I became a part of the Latino organization Peace ran in jail, the other members helped me understand why we were seemingly destined to fail in life, why we continued to repeat cycles that were proven failures, and why we acted in ways that would ensure our being cast out of society and locked in cages like animals.

The first book that gave me a deeper insight into life was called, *Assimilation in American Life: The Role of Race, Religion and National Origins*, written by Milton M. Gordon. In the book, I remember a passage about social structure that read, "Culture, as the social scientist uses the term, refers to the ways of acting and the ways of doing things which are passed down from one generation to the next, not through genetic inheritance but by formal and informal methods of teaching and demonstration." It was with those words that I realized my behavior was heavily influenced by everything I had seen in my household, the school system, and the neighborhood. I began to understand it wasn't me that wanted to behave this way, at least not all of the time.

Up to that point in my life I had never completed a book, much less read a book that spoke to me about my ancestry, my culture, and social influences. As the books became more enlightening, my awareness increased and my attitude began to adjust. I was beginning to rid myself of the destructive behavior that led me to a time and place I could have done without.

Thinking back, it was Peace that introduced me to the person I wanted to be. As much as I hated sitting behind bars, it was the best thing that ever could have happened to me. A few more weeks, months, or years on the streets and I might have been killed or received a life sentence for killing someone. Ironic as it may seem, going to jail saved my life.

About six weeks after I met Peace, I took my GED and passed it with flying colors. I always believed in my intelligence, but I never really applied myself, and didn't really know what I was capable of, until I received that diploma in my hand. It was a testament to the fact that I could make something of my life. When I reached my cell I allowed myself to cry tears of joy. It was the first time in three years that I felt proud of myself. I remember making photocopies of my diploma for my mother, my grandmother, my girlfriends, and anybody else I could think of. I never would have gotten my education if I had stayed on the streets. My brother was on the streets and he didn't have a diploma. Most of my boys didn't have an education. Here I was, a caged up animal, and I had earned an education. I was 19 years old and finally understood that I had a chance to turn my life around for the better. The only way I could thank Peace for saving me was to make sure I did right by him once I returned to the free world.

Success is as addictive as any drug I've ever tried. I immediately began taking business courses in the prison college. I took a job in the paint shop and followed that with a job in the upholstery shop with a lifer named Pops who taught me how

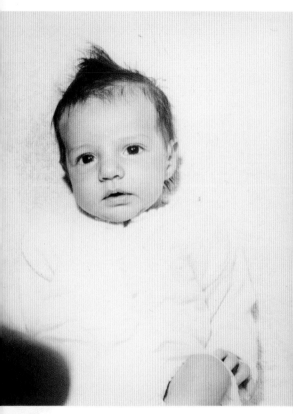

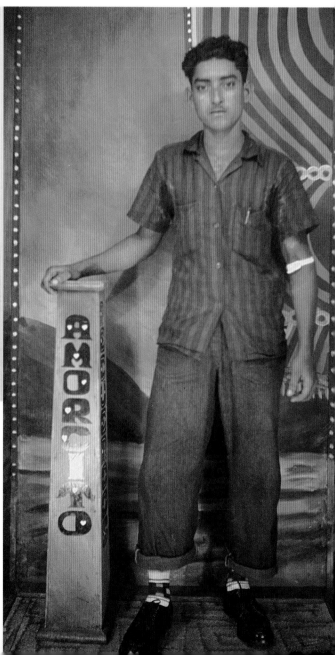

Previous: DJ Disco Wiz, South Bronx
-1976. Background image by Joe Conzo.

Above: DJ Disco Wiz - 1961.

Right: My father Alberto Cedeño.

Top: My grandfather Norberto Cedeño.

Bottom: *La Mano Poderosa*, El Museo del Barrio.

Top: DJ Disco Wiz (center) - four years old, Webster Avenue, Bronx NY, with my first crew.

Bottom: My mother and stepfather - Jenario and Anna Cira Rodriguez.

Top: DJ Disco Wiz - 3rd grade, Saint Simon Stock.

Bottom: DJ Disco Wiz - 9th birthday party with my family in Miami Florida.

BLACK DOOR PRODUCTIONS

PRESENTS

: BATTLE GROUND :

"Grand Master Flash"

"DISCO BEE"

AND THE MELLOW VOICES OF

Keith-Keith : Kid Creole : Mele-Mel

VS

D. J. STARSKY

KOOL A. J. & M. C. KENNY G.

On Friday, February 17th, 1978
From 10:00 p. m. to 5:00 a. m.

at the LUXURIOUS

"XAMACA PLAYHOUSE"

884 Freeman Street : Bronx, N. Y.
Tel. 590-1757
Ask for RAY or CHARLES

DON'T MISS IT...

Ladies $3.00   Gents $4.00

Directions: by Bus No. 31, or 11 to Freeman & Southern Blvd.
by Train No. 2 or 5 to Freeman Street Station.

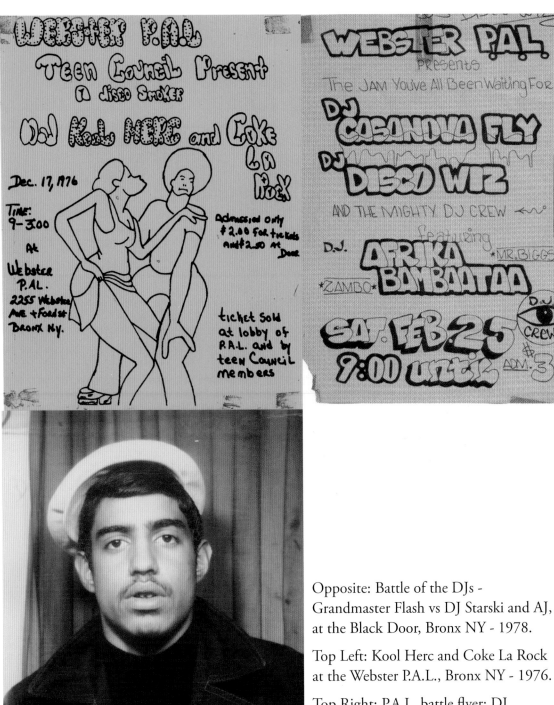

Opposite: Battle of the DJs - Grandmaster Flash vs DJ Starski and AJ, at the Black Door, Bronx NY - 1978.

Top Left: Kool Herc and Coke La Rock at the Webster P.A.L., Bronx NY - 1976.

Top Right: P.A.L. battle flyer: DJ Casanova Fly and DJ Disco Wiz vs. Afrika Bambaataa!!

Bottom: DJ Disco Wiz, Bronx NY - 1975.

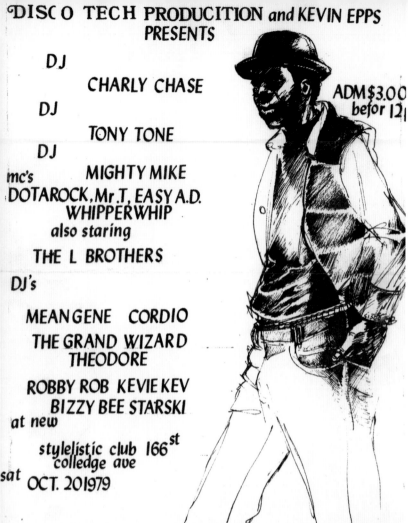

DISCO TECH PRODUCTION and KEVIN EPPS PRESENTS

DJ CHARLY CHASE

DJ TONY TONE

DJ MIGHTY MIKE

mc's DOTAROCK, Mr.T, EASY A.D. WHIPPERWHIP

also staring

THE L BROTHERS

DJ's

MEANGENE CORDIO

THE GRAND WIZARD THEODORE

ROBBY ROB KEVIE KEV BIZZY BEE STARSKI

at new

stylelistic club 166st colledge ave

sat OCT. 20 1979

ADM $3.00 befor 12

Police Athletic League INC.

NEW YORK CITY

TEENAGE MEMBER

No.

Name of Member

Webster-Giannone Community Center

2255 Webster Ave. Center

Bronx, New York 10457

364-5744

Robert M. Morgenthau

PRESIDENT

1976

Top: DJ Charlie Chase, Tony Tone, Mighty Mike, DotaRock, Mr. T, Easy AD, and Whipper Whip featuring: The L Brothers, Mean Gene Cordio, and Grand Wizzard Theodore, with Robby Rob, Kevie Kev, and Busy Bee Starski, Bronx NY - 1979.

Bottom: DJ Disco Wiz, Webster P.A.L. Card, Bronx NY - 1976.

T.M.F. PRODUCTIONS
presents

THE GRAND
MASTER
CASANOVA FLY
and
THE DISCO WIZ
&
D.J. MIGHTY MIKE
featuring
A 1 FEMALE D.J. PAM—BAA—TAA
PLACE TO BE

4529 3RD AVE. BET.
183 & 182
(JUNE 15.....THUR. 7:pm TO 2:AM)
adm $1.00

(JUNE 17.....FRI. 10:pm UNTIL)
adm $2.00

Top Left: DJ Disco Wiz - 1977.

Top Right: DJ Disco Wiz, Bronx NY - 1976.

Bottom: Grandmaster Casanova Fly, DJ Disco Wiz, and Mighty Mike with, Pambaataa - 1977.

Following Spread Left: Diana and DJ Disco Wiz, Roosevelt High School, Bronx NY - 1977.

Following Spread Right: Grandmaster Caz, DJ Disco Wiz, and The Mighty Force Crew: Mighty Mike, Kool Kev, and Pambaataa at the Blue Lagoon, Bronx NY - 1978.

T.M.F. PRODUCTIONS

Proudly Presents ...

THE GRAND MASTER CASANOVA FLY
and
THE DISCO WIZ, MIGHTY MIKE

KOOL KEV and Pambaataa A1 DJs
THE MIGHTY FORCE CREW

AT THE FULLY AIR CONDITIONED
BLUE LAGOON

2324 Webster Ave. and 184th. ST.
SAT. JULY 8, 1978 — SUN. JULY 9, 1978
10:00 until   fee $2.00

EVERY BODY WILL BE THERE !

T.J. PRODUCTIONS
PRESENTS
A BATTLE OF THE DJ'S
AT CLUB 462

East Tremont Ave - Between Park + Wash

MAR 17 ADM=$2.00 10 P.M.

KOOL D.J. TROY
and his sure shot team

D.J. HIMEROCK- DIZZY-DIZ
VS
D.J. CASANOVA FLY
DISCO WIZ

Opposite: Battle of the DJs: Kool DJ Troy, DJ Himerock, Dizzy Diz vs. DJ Casanova
Fly and DJ Disco Wiz at the 462 Club, Bronx NY - 1977.

Above: The Eastside Boys, Valentine Avenue, Bronx NY - 1979.

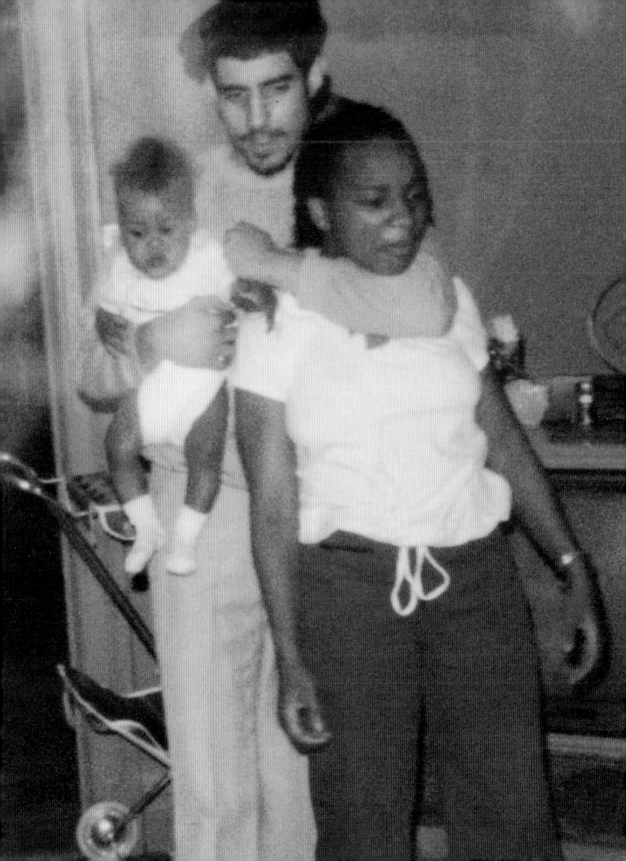

Above: Tammy, DJ Disco Wiz, Crotona Avenue, Bronx NY - 1978.

Opposite: Tammy, DJ Disco Wiz, and Jeanette, Crotona Avenue, Bronx NY - 1978.

Anna Cira Cedeño and DJ Disco Wiz, Coxsackie Correctional - February, 1981.

Top: DJ Disco Wiz, March for Freedom, Coxsackie Correctional - November 22, 1980.

Middle: Ricardo Cedeño and DJ Disco Wiz, Coxsackie Correctional - April, 1981.

Bottom: DJ Disco Wiz, Coxsackie Correctional - summer of 1979.

Above: DJ Disco Wiz and Peace, Coxsackie Correctional - November, 1980.

Opposite Left: Lefty, Joe, and DJ Disco Wiz, Hudson Correctional - 1981.

Opposite Right: DJ Disco Wiz, Coxsackie Correctional - July, 1980.

Opposite Bottom: JDL, DJ Disco Wiz, and Grandmaster Caz - 1982.

Top: DJ Disco Wiz and the Burnside Avenue crew, Poe Park, Bronx NY - 1984.

Bottom: DJ Disco Wiz and the crew on Burnside Avenue - 1984.

Opposite Top: DJ Disco Wiz and Joey Adams, Fordham Road, Bronx NY - 1983.

Opposite Bottom: DJ Disco Wiz and The Cold Crush Brothers, Bronx NY - 1982.

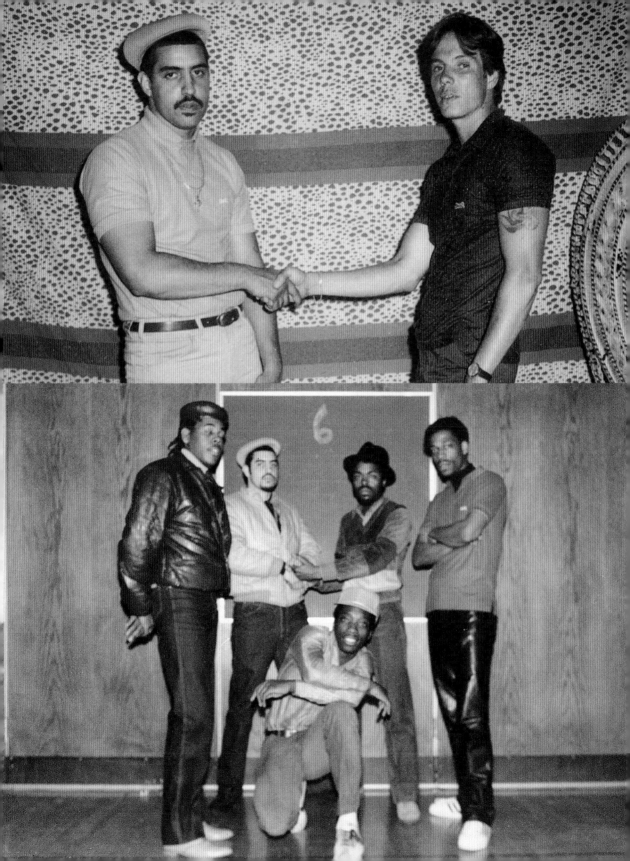

Top Left: DJ Disco Wiz and Solie, 42nd Street - 1984.

Top Right: DJ Disco Wiz and DJ, 42nd Street - 1984.

Bottom: Tata and DJ Disco Wiz, 42nd Street - 1984.

DJ Disco Wiz and the Burnside Avenue crew, 42nd Street - 1983.

Anthony White and DJ Disco Wiz, The University Club, NY - 2000.

Top: DJ Disco Wiz, The University Club, NY - 2000.

Bottom: DJ Disco Wiz and Juan Sahah, The Union League Club, NY - 1989.

Opposite Top: Julio and DJ Disco Wiz, New Year's Eve at The University Club, NY - 1999.

Opposite Middle: Luis and Ricardo Cedeño with our grandmother Virginia - 1997.

Opposite Bottom: Luis and Lizette Cedeño - 1996.

Top Left: Lizette, DJ Disco Wiz, and Grandmaster Caz - 2000.

Bottom Left: DJ Disco Wiz, Afrika Bambaataa Walk of Fame marathon at the point, Bronx NY - 2006. Photo by Joe Conzo.

Above Right: DJ Disco Wiz, b-boy battle - 2006. Photo by Joe Conzo.

Top: My wife Lizette and my daughter Tammy with my four grandchildren, their great grandmother Helen, and cousins - 2007.

Bottom: DJ Disco Wiz, Emmy nominated VH1 Rock Doc, *NY77: The Coolest Year in Hell*. Photo by Corra Films.

Top: DJ Disco Wiz and Afrika Bambaataa, Tools of War Harlem Hop - 2007. Photo by Andrew Sullivan.

Middle: DJ Disco Wiz and Grandmaster Caz, Tools of War Harlem Hop - 2007. Photo by Andrew Sullivan.

Bottom: The Bronx Borough President Adolfo Carrión Jr., Grandmaster Caz, and DJ Disco Wiz. Photo by Joe Conzo.

Opposite : Lizette Fonte-Cedeño - 1994.

Above: Tammy Cedeño.

Following Page: DJ Disco Wiz, the world-famous Apollo Theatre - November 3, 2006.
Photo by Joe Conzo.

to use a commercial sewing machine to upholster furniture. I learned how to do moldings, couch covers, and cut foam for the furniture. It was something I really enjoyed doing, and again, gave me a real sense of achievement every time I looked at a completed piece.

As time went on, I never missed a meeting with the Latino Organization, and after several months I became Treasurer. I'd never truly felt accepted by my people and I felt good to finally be around brothers who cared about me. I had a real sense of pride being around people who cared about their history, cared about education, and cared about the betterment of Latinos inside and outside the wall. Eventually I earned the position of Vice President and found myself mentoring other brothers in the same way Peace had mentored me.

Every meeting was like an awakening. One day I was learning about the Young Lords, the Brown Berets, and the Black Panther Party. The following week I was being educated about people like Delores "Lolita" Lebron Sotomayor and Pedro Albizu Campos, who was educated at Harvard in the early 20th century. I didn't think Puerto Ricans were allowed inside those prestigious halls during the 1980s, much less allowed to graduate in the 1920s. Campos was a Puerto Rican nationalist, but I believe, more than anything else, he was a humanist who believed in protecting the rights of his fellow countrymen.

In 1932 Campos exposed a Rockefeller Institute medical experiment that was responsible for injecting cancer cells into Puerto Rican patients. Dr. Cornelius P. Roads, who headed up the research, had no problem admitting that he killed his patients during these experiments. He was protected by the United States of America and by Rockefeller money, while we were still slaves to American interest. Nothing had changed since the time of Columbus. Campos would later be railroaded by the U.S. justice system and sentenced to 80 years in prison in 1951 for trying to free Puerto Rico from U.S. rule. While incarcerated, he ended up becoming the victim of human radiation experiments headed by the United States Department of Energy. This fact was not revealed until 1994 under the Clinton Administration, nearly 30 years after his death.

I remember reading about female Puerto Rican Nationalist Delores "Lolita" Lebron Sotomayor, who led an attack on the United States House of Representatives on March 1, 1954, to bring attention to Puerto Rican independence. For her role in the uprising, she earned a death sentence, which was later commuted to life in prison.

I also learned about the Young Lords who went from being a violent street gang in Chicago, to being an organization committed to human rights and the liberation of Puerto Rico. I wondered in my jail cell if I might be able to turn my life around and use my influence, street smarts, and newfound book knowledge to help others walk a better path. I was beginning to realize the real power came in helping those who weren't powerful enough to help themselves.

No matter what I was learning at the time, it never seemed to be enough. I felt like I had to make up for lost time. I must have read the Bible about nine times. After I was sent to the bing for 30 days for hitting the guard, I had nothing: no clothes besides my underwear, no sheets on the bed, no visitors, no phone calls, no lights in the cell—even the windows were blacked out, and I still remember the tiny little rays of sunlight that would creep through during the daytime. These were some dark times for me, and the only thing we were allowed to have was the Bible. I studied and read it as though my life depended on it.

I caught myself sitting in my cell a few times, thinking about how fucking ignorant I was the first part of my bid. I finally began to understand what it was the parole board was asking me all those months ago. I made sure to clean up my vocabulary and grammar; it became important to me to not sound like another uneducated Latino from the ghetto. I felt like a boxer training for the match of his life; I was training for the bout that would earn me my freedom.

When I wasn't learning about past leaders and revolutionaries like Campos, Fidel, and Che, I was reading books by Piri Thomas, Claude Brown, and Donald Goines. I related to these books more closely than anything else I was reading. Piri's book showed what it was like to grow up *Down These Mean Streets* of New York. He painted picture perfect stories of how desperate and hopeless life always seemed to be when a racist crew or drug dealer was preying on you at every corner. It was the kind of book that made me realize that that no matter how hard society tried to fix its ills, there would never be the right answer at the right time. Why else would I have to face some of the very same things Piri faced twenty or so years earlier?

I remained in a position of power as Vice President in the group for several months, until my transfer to the minimum-security facility, Hudson Correctional. Everyone told me my transfer meant I was one step closer to going home, but I didn't want to get my hopes up only to have them later crushed. But the truth was, you were either sent further upstate or closer to home, and I had just gone in the right direction for the first time in years.

When I arrived at Hudson, I immediately saw the difference between a maximum and a minimum prison. Hudson was made up of cottages spread throughout a campus-like setting. It was peaceful and tranquil, completely unlike the never ending walls, the guards in the towers, and the lockdowns at Coxsackie. It felt a lot less like being locked up, and a lot more like being rehabilitated. When I walked around the campus I thought long and hard about what it was that had brought me to this place and time. I had finally earned something better for myself, and the fact that I knew what got me there told me I might be able to sustain it this time.

There are pitfalls at every corner in prison; it's very hard to find an upside to it all. It's survival of the fittest to the 10th power. Coxsackie opened my eyes to the harsh realities of prison life and I saw enough to make sure I'd keep prison as a last option once I was freed. I saw people being raped in prison, extorted for their money, and brutally beaten both by the guards and fellow inmates. I saw an inmate murdered and other inmates shanked and cut just for looking at the wrong person the wrong way. Make no mistake about it: the weak are preyed upon in prison and if you aren't strong enough to survive on the inside you'll end up washing another man's underwear, sucking his dick, or taking it in the ass. When you enter prison you either fight to survive or you get fucked to survive, neither of which is a very appealing option. It gives true meaning to the saying "Don't do the crime if you can't do the time."

After being systematically programmed at Coxsackie to eat, sleep, and shit on their clock, I didn't know how to act with all the free time I was given at Hudson. I could sleep when I wanted to, shit when I wanted to, and take as long as I wanted to wipe my ass. Such small things in life, that were stripped along with my dignity, were slowly being returned to me, and my right to manhood came back with it. It was an awkward feeling at first, and I understand now why some people who do 20 or 30 years in maximum security prisons are never able to acclimate to life on the outside.

I only spent about six months at Hudson Correctional and in that time I eagerly awaited my opportunity to be placed in front of the board again, and tell them all about my transformation. When I walked into the room to face the parole board, I was eager to tell them who I had become, and I was confident in the steps I had taken towards rehabilitation. I shook the hands of the board members, the people who held my future life in their hands, and I smiled at them to let them know I was no longer the angry young Latino male they read about in their briefing reports.

An older gentleman started the conversation by asking, "How are you Mr. Cedeño?"

I answered, "I'm happy to be here. How are you?"

It was night and day compared to my last visit to a parole board. I actually had a lot to say and no chip on my shoulder about spending the last four-and-a-half years in prison.

"What have you been up to Mr. Cedeño?"

"Well, since the last time I've been in front of the board. I got my High School Equivalency Diploma. I've been taking college courses and learning several trades."

"Tell us about the trades you've picked up," he asked.

"I took a painting trade and learned how to be a professional painter. I've also earned a certificate for professional upholsterer which is something I really enjoy doing. I've learned how to use my hands to make something out of nothing and in that, I've learned about being productive." I couldn't get the words out fast enough and as I spoke I tried hard to remember all the things I had learned and accomplished. "Since being sent to Hudson I've been working with the community activists here. Trying to make sure others around me see their potential after being freed from prison."

One of the members calmly asked, "We see you've been in trouble in jail Mr. Cedeño, what was your turning point?"

"I can't really answer a specific time or day, sir. But eventually I just found peace with my mistakes. I no longer want to be a negative influence in my community. I want to go home and do positive things." I thought long and hard about telling them about my introduction to Peace and the fact that I joined a Latino Organization but I heard that it often backfired on brothers trying to get sprung from prison. I didn't feel the need to jeopardize myself and be labeled as a radical. I saw no reason to give them that information and have it harm me, so I kept it to myself.

However the words coming out of my mouth were sincere. I had done enough damage in my community. I had hurt enough people and I had paid the price for all of those things. I was ready to go home and eager to set things straight with my family. What I was saying to the parole board wasn't scripted. It came from my heart and I believe the board saw the real transformation I had over the last eighteen months. And they must be so used to dealing with convicts, criminals, and con men that they can smell the bullshit a mile away. I'm sure a great deal of them can see sincerity as well. If I had any chance of gaining my freedom this time, I had to be sure to keep things honest. It was something I never would have understood less than a year earlier.

I didn't even wait for them to ask me the question. "Sir, if the board sets me free I know I will be a productive member of society. I miss my girlfriend and the child I left behind. I miss my mother and my brother. I want to go home and get a job. I want to get married one day and raise a family. I want to be happy. But most importantly I want to put this experience behind me. I'll never forget about my mistakes, but I want to put them behind me and start fresh."

I started to ramble when one of the men interrupted me. I wondered if I had done enough to gain my freedom. Had I been too honest? Had I said too much?

"Mr. Cedeño, we believe you've been rehabilitated and are ready to be freed. You're going home," he said.

It took me a few minutes to understand the words he was saying. After being incarcerated for so long, after thinking I'd never go home again, I couldn't immediately comprehend I was free. When I finally realized what he said, I shook my head in disbelief. "Is it OK if I shake your hand?" I asked.

When they gave me the green light, I jumped up and shook their hands and thanked them profusely. I'll never forget their faces. Three white males and a black woman had given me back my life. It was December 1981, and I had just received the greatest Christmas present any man, woman, or child could have ever given me. I had just been given the gift of freedom.

When I went back to my cell I thought about the last time my mother had come to visit me in jail. It was right before I'd been sent to Hudson and my mother was very ill. Seeing her that sick made me think back to all the times I thought she was going to die. It was tough for me to see my mother like that. Even at her weakest she still made the eight-hour trek to Coxsackie to visit me. When I looked over at my mother standing in line, holding a shopping bag with food, waiting to be allowed to walk to the table, my heart broke into a million pieces. It took every bit of strength in me not to breakdown crying in front of the prison population, but inside it killed me. I wondered what I would do if my mother died before I came home to be by her side in her moment of need. I never wanted to feel like that again.

When my mother got to the table I could no longer hold back the tears. I began to cry, grabbed my mother's hand, and said, "Listen, I will never come back to this fucking place. I promise you Mami, I will never come back here." I told my mother over and over again how sorry I was. That day all of those emotions, all of the regret over the pain I had caused my mother, came flooding out of me. "Mami, I'm sorry I embarrassed you. I'm so sorry you had to feel bad about having a son like me." I told her I had changed and promised her she would never have to visit me in jail again.

It was a promise I planned to keep. I had run for so long that I finally grew tired. I ran from the pain, I ran from the truth, I ran from everything even when I didn't know what I was running from—but I wasn't going to run anymore.

Track 8: You Gotta Do Your Thing

I left prison on February 9, 1982, after spending more than four years of my life behind bars. The New York State Department of Corrections gave me $40.00 in cash, a check for $122.19, and an Amtrak train ticket back to New York City so that I could begin my life as a free man. On the train ride home I enjoyed the peacefulness of the train ride, but felt an uneasy tension about returning to the block. Even though I tried my best not to show it, jail had broke me; I let a few tears stream down my face while I stared out the window. I wasn't sure how I was going to avoid the streets once they started calling, but I had more going for me now than ever before. I hoped that my newfound knowledge would sustain me in the concrete jungle.

When you're in jail, you dream about the day you come home and you envision the parades of friends and parties that will welcome you back. When I arrived at Grand Central Station there was nothing there to greet me but a payphone. I called my mother and when she heard my voice, she cried so much that she could barely give me directions to her new place on Gun Hill Road. When I hung up, I tried to hail a cab but couldn't catch one to save my life so I called back to ask my brother how to get to their apartment.

When I finally got on the D train everyone and everything seemed very small including the train I was on. I felt totally out of place and an overwhelming sense of loneliness, and when I entered my mother's apartment, our conversation was very limited. My brother barely had two words to say to me and he didn't seem happy to see me at all. A lot of my friends and family members were not so thrilled to see me, and even though they put up a good front, I could see right through all of the fake shit. You see, while I was away my reputation had taken on a life of its own, and now I had become a scary motherfucker who had finally been set free. People just didn't know how to approach me. I was always a private person so no one knew about the positive changes in my life while I was away; to them my street resume was first and foremost.

So much had changed in four years. My mother was now remarried to a man named Jenario Rodriguez. He had come into our lives after my father died; he was always very respectful to my mother and treated Rico and me well. Seeing him again reminded me of when I was 14 years old, when he used to take me to work with him at his fruit stand in La Marqueta, the Spanish market in East Harlem that ran from 110th Street to 116th and Park Avenue. It was more than my own father ever did.

I soon learned that Jeanette had given birth to another child, a son named Jason, but was also strung out on drugs. The first time I saw her again, at her apartment on Longfellow Avenue in the Bronx, she kissed me on the mouth and I was caught off guard. She smiled and told me she needed to kiss me to know that she no longer had any feelings for me. I understood. I was saddened by her condition, but even with all of her problems, she still had a good heart.

Jeanette's mother Helen was now raising Tammy in Mt. Vernon, New York. It was an arrangement that came with its own set of problems. Helen made it clear that I would not be able to play a role in my daughter's life and even threatened to call the police when I requested to see my daughter. I saw Tammy only one time, when Jeanette brought her to meet me for lunch on Fordham Road. My daughter was now five years old, so beautiful, and smart. Tammy was told that she could never mention seeing me to her grandmother, that's how bad it was. To this day I'm not sure how Helen found out, but Jeanette got into mad drama over it, and it was the last time I saw my little girl.

The block was the same as I had left it. Some shit never changed—but not for my brother Caz. Things had changed for him in a big way. He was now the captain of the Cold Crush Brothers, which consisted of Almighty KG, JDL, Easy AD, DJ Tony Tone, and DJ Charlie Chase. He was putting out albums, touring the world, and had just returned from Japan after promoting *Wild Style*, the first Hip Hop movie, which was written and directed by Charlie Ahearn.

I remember going over to visit Caz at the same apartment we used to hang out in as kids at 181st Street and Creston Avenue. Damn! I hadn't seen him since 1978, and even though we seemed worlds apart, we were happy to see each other. We kicked it for a minute and at one point he told me that if I wanted to, I could get back down with him and his new crew. I just smiled and joked that DJing was the last thing on my mind. I was coming home to a whole new world that I knew nothing about and had no desire whatsoever for Hip Hop. At that moment in time I truly believed that I had missed the boat by going away and didn't want to play catch up, but I appreciated Caz's gesture of support.

I began parole in February 1982. When I reported to my parole officer, I realized that I wasn't going to be looked at as a newly educated human being. I was going to be seen as an ex-convict, a screw-up, and a street cat who would end up being sent back. One of the stipulations of being on parole meant I had to find a job fast. I filled out application after application and each time I checked the box that said convicted felon, I felt very exposed. It was discouraging to put in so many applications and not receive a single phone call. After several months of failing to find a job, I began to argue my position with my parole officer. I couldn't quite grasp how the fuck he didn't get it, and it was at that point in time that I made a conscious decision that the next few jobs I applied for I'd *forget* to check that little fucking box. I had nothing to lose; so what if they found out I was a convict— at least I'd get a few paychecks in before they realized I'd gotten over. Not only would I forget to tell my potential employer I was an ex-con, I would stop telling the entire world about my jail history. From that moment on I very rarely, if ever, told anyone about my past.

One day my mother told me that her friend said I should drop by her job, that they were always hiring extra help. I walked into a private club called the Union League Club on East 37th Street and Park Avenue. I asked the person at the employee's entrance for an application and as I filled it out I stared intensely at the section of the application where it asked, "Have you ever been convicted of a felony?" I checked the box under no for the first time in my life and walked out wondering if I had made the right choice. I would receive my answer several days later when I got the call to come in for an interview.

Landing my first position as an on-call extra waiter felt like a major victory. It was a demeaning occupation but it was honest work. I remember looking around and seeing old black men serving the upper-echelon white people. The shit seemed very down-south racist to me, but for the sake of keeping the job I swallowed my pride and made the best of the situation. I got close to some of the older waiters who had been down since the Pullman Railroad days of the Roaring Twenties. These dudes were some real OGs. One guy named Leo took a liking to me. He used to call me young buck and schooled me on all the proper dining room etiquette. Shit, I didn't have any idea what fork went where, that you serve from the right and pick up plates from the left, that red wine goes with meat and game, and that white wine goes with fish and poultry. I was being placed in finishing school without even realizing it.

One day the captain told me I was too *white* to serve the members at the club. How the fuck could I be too white if I was a Spanish kid from the Boogie Down Bronx? Regardless, I knew at that point that I had to politic my way into a situation that benefited me. I was always interested in what the guys in the kitchen were doing. It was the greatest dance of organized chaos I'd ever seen, and something about that appealed to me. I started talking to the chef every time I got a chance.

I always made sure to catch him when he wasn't in the middle of doing a million things and make small talk with him, or just try to make him laugh. I figured I'd talk my way into a position in the kitchen.

"Yo chef, you don't have a job for me in the kitchen man? I'm a hard worker chef," I shouted out one day.

"Work harder and talk less then," he shouted back.

"Yo chef, come on man, put me to work. I need a steady gig and medical benefits. Why don't you give me a shot behind that hot ass stove?"

"Kid, you wouldn't know what to do back here."

Little did this motherfucker know that five years earlier I had spent nearly a year working the mess hall at Rikers. Not to mention I had to do most of the cooking at home since the age of eight, after my mother got sick. I even baked some cakes on the side for extra cash.

Four or five weeks after fucking with the chef every chance I got, he called me over one day. "Hey Lou come over here."

"What's up chef?"

"Were you serious about working with us in the kitchen?"

"Yeah man, you crazy, you got a job for me chef?"

"Shhh, be quiet. Would you mind starting out washing dishes?"

"Chef, I'll do whatever it takes. I'll wash dishes. I'll mop the floor. Is it steady work with benefits?"

"Yes of course, full time, forty hours a week with benefits."

Someone else's misfortune became my career beginnings. The Ecuadorian kid who got fired for not taking his job seriously opened the door for me to take over a smooth gig cleaning the small intimate dining rooms where private power lunches were held. This was a different world all together, with its own set of rules, and I began mapping out my culinary career. When one of the old cooks retired, my new mentor Juan, the assistant chef who had taken me under his wing, brought me into the kitchen. He taught me everything I would have learned had I gone to any of the top culinary schools. Only in New York would I be trained in classic French cuisine by a Dominican guy from Washington Heights. I would go from dishwasher, to food prep, and eventually to being a Sous Chef, but the road would prove to be long and extremely difficult.

It was the early 80s. I was 21 years old and I finally had job security and was making good money. If you had seen me in the streets at that time you would've sworn I was hustling. The money I was bringing in allowed me to stay fresh with my gear, and I was back to rocking the latest Kangol hats, sheepskin coats, and shell-toe Adidas with matching track suits—the whole nine. Fresh to death was the motto I'd always lived by. Although I looked like I was selling drugs, I was in fact getting up at 4:00 in the morning to work hard for a living. It was hard for me to believe this was really my life. Sometimes when my alarm clock rang it startled me and made me think I was back in the slammer.

If there was one thing I really missed, it was being with a woman after so long! I was sent away as a kid, but had come home a man. I immediately embarked on a non-stop rampage of tapping out new pieces almost every week. I was now cock-fucking diesel, and ripped, with a 28-inch waist and a strong motherfucking back. Shit, long gone were the days of my hands substituting for a good piece of pussy.

Although I wasn't hanging out hard in the streets, I'd still link up from time to time with my man Caz and a crew from over in the Burnside area of the Bronx. There was a little clique of girls that included a young cutie named Lillian, who everybody called Tata. Caz was dating her sister Lucy; she had other sisters named Cuca and Olga and a brother named Rick that we all called Slick Rick. The first time I hooked up with Tata was one night after hanging out with her and some of the crew at Skate Key on 149th Street. At the time, she was messing around with a cat named SK. I was cool with him, but Tata and I gravitated towards one another, and the flirting quickly led to our spending the night together. From that moment on, she became my main girl and Burnside Avenue became my new home.

I had a lot of respect in the neighborhood. The boys on Burnside had just lost one of their most feared crew members to the penitentiary, a dude named Santana. Santana had a reputation much like mine, a stick-up kid who was about his business. Now he was inside experiencing all the things I'd just left behind while I became the person who was respected and feared in the neighborhood.

Tata had a son named Christopher who was less than a year old. It was my first introduction to playing stepdad to another man's child and it filled a void for me, since I was not able to be a part of my daughter's life. Now that I had a makeshift family, it was time for me move out of my mother's home.

Rico and I were not getting along. For some reason he'd forgotten about all the years I'd spent keeping him out of trouble growing up. I tried my best to keep the peace but it just didn't work out that way. Although I loved my brother and tried having a relationship with him, he disrespected me every chance he got. He got into this little habit of calling me a fucking jailbird, especially in front of his friends, after a few beers. This shit was not going to fly with me. One day we came down to blows in my mother's apartment. When the smoke cleared we'd destroyed the bedroom entirely. Eight months after hitting the streets, I moved out of my mother's apartment and in with Tata and her son on 181st Street and Tiebout Avenue.

Tata was a third generation welfare recipient, but she was a sweet girl, and I had no problems being the breadwinner of the household. Little did I know at the time, I was about to make a lot more cash. Over the next two years I learned how to be more responsible, how to be a father, and how to be a young professional, but an opportunity presented itself to me one day—and it was an offer I couldn't refuse.

It was now the mid 80s and I had become cool with this Columbian cat named Carlos at work. He saw my street swagger and even though I was working in an Ivy League environment I was coming into work with a lot of jewelry, always dressed to impress. It wasn't cheap maintaining my look and it was probably one of the reasons he felt like he could approach me with a money making proposition. He told me he had a crazy cocaine connection in Queens and that I could make a lot of money pushing weight for him.

Realistically, the nine-to-five wasn't cutting it for me, even though I had a good job. Everyone I knew had a side hustle; mine was slinging white powder. Within weeks, I was running a coke route for him, making deliveries. It was straight cocaine. I sold grams, eightballs, and ounces. I never realized how many guys at my job had a cocaine habit and I was now collecting my paycheck along with three-quarters of most of the crew's pay. For them it meant that all of their overtime, hard work, and dealing with all the bullshit on the job was for nothing more than some drugs.

Me? As I began to learn the distribution system, any fear I had was quickly overshadowed by my excitement. Being an everyday Joe Schmoe just wasn't cutting it for me. I needed the rush to know I was alive. Now that I was out of jail, and out of Hip Hop, I had no motivation, no inspiration. Selling coke, making money, and not getting caught gave me that thrill. I had a new purpose in life.

I traded in my subway tokens for the keys to a brand new candy apple red Audi 5000. It was a 100% show of status. I hadn't been home for more than two years and now I was a fly dude in my early 20s working on Park Avenue with his own apartment and a brand new European sports car. I had the world by the balls.

The only problem I had was trying to decide whether working as a chef was even necessary. It was Carlos who explained why I needed to keep my day job. "You gotta understand something Lou. We're allowed to have cars and nice apartments and money because we got jobs, but the second we don't have jobs anymore, people are gonna ask where the fuck we're getting our shit from. You don't ever want anyone asking that question. The moment they do, you go back to jail."

I stayed focused on the hustle and carried on accordingly. Everything was running smoothly until Juan pulled me to the side one day and said, "Yo Lou, people are saying you are selling coke on the job."

I stared at him without saying anything, trying to figure out if he wanted to cop some blow or if he was accusing me of being a drug dealer. He continued, "I don't want to get involved with this Lou, *sabes que yo te quiero como un hijo*. I don't need you to answer me, but if you're selling drugs, *yo quiero que tú dejes esa mierda* because they are investigating you."

Fuck me…an investigation. Was someone watching me? Were they talking to my customers? Was someone gonna rat me out? I felt a thousand pounds of pressure on me. Juan treated me like his son and regardless of what he thought of my side job, he was still looking out for me.

As I thought about the situation, I realized that the one thing I was not ready to do was go back to jail. I called in sick for a few days and sat in my apartment, deeply paranoid and wondering if the cops were going to break down my door and haul my stupid ass back to jail. I decided to close up shop. There were a bunch of dudes I knew dying to take over my route anyway so I sold one of them the remaining product, the packaging materials, the scale, my route, and introductions to the people he needed to know. Once that was done, I washed my hands and walked away.

At the time I wasn't sure if I was doing the right thing. Not only did I stand to lose a lot of money, but I had also taken on a habit of my own, without even noticing. While packing up some product late into the night I just said, "Fuck it," and took a hit of coke. Before I knew it, it was daylight and I had spent all night packing and sniffing, while things with Tata seemed to go from bad to worse.

When we first got together, we became good friends and lovers. She was my around the way girl, always fly, street swagger and all. We were both young and in love, with no real worries, but her jealous nature lead to our downfall. I have been called a flirt and a player but once you get past my rough edges, I'm just a nice guy. I treated all her people the same and that used to drive her crazy. Soon enough the fights began to outnumber the good times as her jealousy just grew out of control. Once that happened I didn't need to be in the relationship anymore.

It was time for a fresh start. I packed up my shit up and bounced 15 blocks away to 196th Street, off Jerome Avenue, in the Kingsbridge section of the Bronx. That was ill fucking territory at the time. Drug spots were springing up all over the place and a lot of screwface motherfuckers were doing their thing on those streets. For the most part, no one fucked with me. I looked the part, so I didn't really have to deal with any bullshit.

I became focused making money the legal way. I took a second job in Fort Lee, New Jersey, at a kosher restaurant, and continued on my career path of becoming a chef. Just as I began to settle into my new lifestyle, Tata popped back into the picture. I decided to give her another chance and she moved in with me, but soon enough we were back to the same old bullshit. After less than a year we broke up for good and I returned to my first love: Hip Hop. In the mid-80s I picked up my first pair of brand new turntables. Hip Hop was entering its golden years with the emergence of Public Enemy, Boogie Down Productions, the Juice Crew, Eric B. and Rakim, Run-DMC, and L.L. Cool J. I was now a fan of the music and the culture, standing on the outside looking in.

These days were some of the calmest in my life. This was the first time in my life I was completely liberated, freed from the abusive father, the prison system, the crazy-ass girlfriend, and the drug habit. On April 17, 1984, I received a Certificate of Release from the state of New York; because of my ability to keep gainful employment, my parole was cut from five years to two-and-a-half and I was officially discharged. I was finally free.

I felt very conflicted. On one hand I worked very hard as a Sous Chef and tried my best to live out that American Dream, but my everyday reality was survival at whatever cost. It was difficult for me to shake off that jailhouse swagger; no matter how good things were going I would always apply that dog-eat-dog mentality. Even though I was now part of the real world, I wasn't free inside. By all appearances I was the picture of success for all to see and envy, but behind closed doors I struggled with regrets and never fully appreciated all the gifts I had been given. I would just go through the motions with no feelings at all.

In 1984, I met Arcy, when she started working in the accounting office at the Union League Club. She would come up into the kitchen wearing sexy business suits and would flirt and pester us for special food off the menu. She was Puerto Rican and fine as hell—and she knew it. All the cooks, and even the Executive Chef, used to go gaga over her every word. I never paid her much attention, I would always act too busy to be bothered, but I would sometimes catch her looking at me as she left the kitchen floor. My partner Juan used to tease me about her when she was around—he even gave her a nickname, "La China," because she had a flat ass.

One day she stopped at my station and I kicked some intense game to her as she blushed and turned red around the ears. The flirting soon turned into a dinner date, and it didn't take long for us to become a couple. From time to time I would stay at her place in Long Island and learned that she was a soft-spoken good girl from a good family who loved the bad boy in me. She was the first girl who attempted to change me from what some would say were my street ways, and I fell in love with her and her little girl Emily straight away. Arcy was the first woman to introduce me to something other than a night at the movies, dinner, or a Hip Hop jam. She knew I had potential to leave some of that hood mentality behind, and ours was the first healthy relationship I had ever had. She was my first true love and I dared to dream beyond my reach with her. After about a year of dating, Arcy and I began to discuss marriage, and I began looking at engagement rings.

Unfortunately Tata wasn't out of the picture. I was in love with Arcy but Tata was my girl from way back, and we had a long history together. One night she came by the crib, talking about how bad she missed me and wanted me. One thing led to another and before I knew it, we were all over each other. Then Arcy knocked on the door and Tata let her in. I could tell by the look on Arcy's face that she was destroyed. Little did I know, I was being played by Tata—I believed she really loved me but truth be told she didn't want to see me with Arcy. That night I lost them both.

It was right around this time that the crack epidemic swept the streets of New York. My neighborhood became a huge strip for crack whores; it was sad to drive home past all these young girls who were once beautiful, now all dried up and walking the hoe stroll. The area was so dangerous you couldn't leave your car without waking up to broken glass and half your shit taken. Crack turned once normal people into unrecognizable zombies.

My childhood friend Karim ended up strung out and homeless in the street, disgustingly dirty, without shoes, and looking like some hobo. It was 1989 and we barely recognized one another. "How the fuck did Karim end up like this?" I remember thinking to myself. He never did any jail time; he was so talented that he was even scouted for minor league baseball teams, his fastball was that nasty; *Coño* if anyone of us was going to make it, it would've been him. Seeing him in the street broke my heart. I gave him a fist full of money and broke down into tears. "What a fucked up world we live in," I said to myself as I walked away.

He wasn't the only one sucking on the glass dick. My younger cousins Junior and Millie were strung out too. Crack turned Junior into a three-time felon who stole everything he could from everyone he knew, including his mother and my poor grandmother. I made sure that motherfucker didn't know where I lived and stayed clear of his path. In the 80s and early 90s New York was like the Wild West and I always worried about the day I'd have to pull out my joint and use it again.

A few years after losing Tata and Arcy, I met a girl named Jennifer in my neighborhood. Jenny was the typical Latina in the Bronx with a hard story to tell. Only 18 years old, she was trying to raise her two boys on welfare. Both kids had different fathers and both fathers were in jail, one for murder and one for robbery charges. She was living from apartment to apartment and had lost custody of her children, being unable to support them. Her oldest son, Nicholas, lived with her mother on Burnside Avenue and her younger son, Jonathon, lived with his grandmother somewhere else in the Bronx.

We got serious after about a week. I made her a set of keys and told her she could live with me. My apartment was dope. Most of the women that came to my crib thought I had a girl decorate the place, but the truth was I liked nice things, and I had really hooked the place up. I could pretty much do it all. I could cook, sew, iron, and clean. I never relied on anyone for anything. I had no choice; I learned to take care of everything since I was a kid, from hooking up my own spot to always looking fly. It was a three-bedroom apartment fully furnished. I even had my own washer and dryer.

After about a month I asked her to bring her kids to live with us. She told me the grandmothers didn't trust her enough to let her have the kids but I persisted, and soon enough, the kids were living with us. After being with Jenny for about a year, she told me that she was pregnant with my child. Since I never had the chance to be a real father to my daughter Tammy, I was ecstatic about being a dad again, and I played to the fact that she wanted a daughter. "I only make little girls," I said with a smile.

I enjoyed everything about the pregnancy process and took care of all of her needs while she was carrying my child. I thought back to when I was 16, doing the same thing for Tammy's mother, and I felt at peace. I was finally going to have a child that I could raise from a newborn into adulthood. I couldn't have been any happier.

On November 12, 1988, my daughter Ashley was born in Jacobi Hospital in the Bronx. I cried like a baby when I saw her little head pop out. Nothing brought me more comfort and more joy. I had played stepdad to Christopher, Emily, Nicolas, and Jonathan, all while never being able to see my own little girl Tammy, and now I was being given another opportunity to be a father and do it right this time. All I could do was cry tears of joy as I held little Ashley in my arms.

One night a couple of years later, Jenny and I were sitting up late, talking about where we wanted to go next with our relationship. I had already asked her to marry me and given her an engagement ring. Even though the boys weren't mine, I treated them like my sons and I considered them all my kids. We were in a good place but as the discussion continued, Jenny started to cry uncontrollably. In a cracked voice, she said, "Louie, I have to tell you something but I'm scared. I'm so scared."

"It's OK, I'm here for you. No matter what," I said uncertain if I'd be able to keep that promise. I figured she was going to tell me she cheated on me so I braced myself.

"I've been sleeping with Jonathon's father," she said.

I took a deep breath while my heart sunk deep into my stomach.

"I've been sleeping with him for years."

I was at a loss for words and trying to decipher what she was saying. The anger building in me made it hard for me to understand what she was really saying. I wasn't ready for the next sentence...

"Ashley isn't yours."

Fuuuuuuuuuuuuuuuuuuuuuuuuuuuuck.

I wanted to kill this bitch but I couldn't. My heart literally stopped beating. I could no longer hear anything she was saying. I couldn't feel anything. I was dead and I wanted to stay dead. The little girl I had held, kissed, hugged, and played with for two years was no longer my child. I had just lost my little girl again.

After everything I did for this chick—bringing her into my home and helping her get her kids back—this is how she paid me back! Man, I was played like the stupid motherfucker that I was. I should have known better than to try to save someone who didn't give a shit about being saved. I fucking hated her for what she did to me. The only person I thought was in my corner had just stabbed me in the back.

Although I stayed with Jenny after she confessed to me, I was no longer with Jenny. I was embarrassed about being played to that extent, and I kept that shit a secret from everyone I knew. I still loved Ashley with all my heart, but it was so hard knowing what I now knew. I understood that one day Jenny and I would separate and that I'd lose Ashley forever.

The pain in my heart was unbearable.

Just when I thought things couldn't get any worse, I received a phone call from my childhood friend Solie. It was New Year's Eve 1991, and he was calling to tell me that his older brother, one of my closest friends, Anthony (Tony Rome) Nieto, had just gotten his head blown off by a rival drug dealer on 181st Street and Morris Avenue. The news was another devastating blow and I had no one to turn to, not God, not my mother, not my family, not Jenny, no one. So I did the only thing I could: cocaine and alcohol to dull the pain.

That night, around 3:00 am, as I left the Palladium on 14th Street, I began to feel my heart beating out of my chest. I immediately knew that something was terribly wrong. Jenny took one look at me, and started screaming. My cocaine binge had brought me to the point of overdose. Jenny tried to call an ambulance but I managed to mutter the words, "No cops." As my throat started to close, she called my drug dealer who told her to give me some milk and put me in a cold shower. As I stood in the shower, I remember thinking every breath could be my last. At the same time I could hear Jenny in the next room sniffing whatever was left of my supply.

Shit. What the fuck am I doing here?

It was at that moment that I realized I'd probably live to see another day, but all I truly wanted was to die.

Track 9: Once We Have Togetherness

For some people, overdosing on cocaine and nearly losing your life would be considered hitting rock bottom, but after experiencing a lifetime of pain, it was just another step on the path of self-destruction and there was no end in sight. That night would prove to have a domino effect on my life, and just as the ice cold water ran down the drain, my world would soon follow.

I was living in a junkie's paradise. We'd throw dinners or birthday parties just to get high. Fight nights at the crib with my boys became coke events. All roads led to those little white lines laid out on a table, and soon the habit became too expensive to maintain. I was always late on the rent. Shit, all my bills were either late or never paid. I even sold my DJ equipment and turntables to cover a drug debt. It was one of the toughest things I had to do, but somehow I had the sense to hang onto my vinyl. It was the only link left to my childhood dreams.

I hooked up with some Dominican cats in the neighborhood and began pushing weight again, as if I had never left the game. My heart turned colder than it had been in years and I became ruthless, walking around with two or three guns ready for whatever popped off. I'm not even sure how I managed to hang on to my day job because my reality was staying up all night, driving around with no license, coked up and drunk while packing a 9 mm Sig-Sauer and a .40 loaded with black, rhino-armor-piercing bullets. It was a miracle I was never pulled over.

One Sunday afternoon in 1991, while watching a New York Giants game with a bunch of fellas at my crib, we ran out of soda. I told the guys to keep eating their pizza and I'd make a quick run to the corner bodega. I'd made this run a million times and felt safe leaving the guns at home, but as I walked down the hill towards the store, I heard a voice crack the air, "Yo, gimme your shit."

I was rocking a few gold chains and thought the guy was joking around. I couldn't see someone trying to rob me in my own hood, so at that moment the seriousness of the situation just didn't register. But when I looked into the guy's eyes, I saw he had this crazed look about him and it was then that I realized he was holding an automatic handgun and pointing it at my chest.

"Yo motherfucker, stop fucking around and gimme me your shit."

As the adrenaline kicked in, everything seemed to happen in slow motion. "Get the fuck out of here!" I shouted as he began to point the gun towards my head. As I pushed the gun away, he let off a deafening shot. I felt the warm blood splatter against my face and neck. When I looked at my hand I saw that two of my fingers were just kind of hanging there. The blast left a gaping hole in my left hand.

Right before the gun went off, I was throwing a punch with my right hand and caught him with a knockout blow. I watched him fall in between two parked cars. I wanted to stomp him into the fucking concrete but with blood gushing out of both sides of the wound, I knew I had to get medical attention quickly. I was starting to feel woozy, faint, and lethargic.

The commotion had sent a bunch of neighborhood cats running down the block to come to my aid and the gunmen got up and took off running when he saw the group coming after him. A guy named Fredo, who lived in my building, wrapped my hand in his shirt and raced me to North Central Hospital. I saw my life flash before my eyes a few times and that only made matters worse.

Wow, this little mother fucker tried to kill me for a few chains. Ain't that a bitch?

At the hospital I was rushed into surgery. The doctor said, "I'm sorry, but this is going to hurt." Without anesthesia, he began to remove all the dead skin that was burnt by gunpowder when I was shot at point blank. I spent a week in ICU, and did eight hard weeks of intense physical therapy. I had to learn how to use my hand again, and sometimes I felt like I would never recover from the injuries.

At the time I thought it was a bullshit robbery, but after the shooting, the drug dealers I worked with began avoiding me, leading me to believe that possibly they had something to do with it. I had earned a reputation as a take-no-shit dealer and the Dominicans I was working with began to fear me. My gut instinct told me the attempted robbery was really an attempted murder and I wasn't happy about these motherfuckers trying to take me out. Soon enough simply ignoring their existence turned into exchanging looks that could kill. A lot of the drug spots were in my hood and I had to see these guys all the time, so I made sure I kept my .40 loaded and off safety at all times. If they made another attempt on my life, I wasn't going be throwing punches, I was going be throwing bullets at these bitches.

I could no longer work as a chef and lost my job. I was denied receiving disability three times; it was believed that because of my vocational training I could work with one hand. The real problem was that I was in the neighborhood a lot more than I wanted to be, but as fate would have it, one of the drug spots was raided shortly afterwards. They must have believed it was set up by me as retribution, but I didn't have a fucking thing to do with it. Even in my most fucked up days, I always lived my life by the code of the streets, something these fucking *plátanos* would never understand.

Right around this time, Jenny received a call that her brother had been killed in a traffic accident on the New Jersey Turnpike while changing a tire. The day of the funeral we went back to my place with about 20 or 30 people from Jenny's family coming over to our place to mourn. As we pulled up to the block, it must have looked like I was rolling up with a bunch of my boys looking for trouble.

I went to sleep late that night, exhausted from the emotional toll all of this was taking on me. When I woke up the next morning I discovered that my car had been destroyed. It was a brand new Ford Taurus SHO and it had been completely worked over. All the tires were slashed, every window was busted, and the interior had been fucked up as well.

When I went back upstairs to call a few friends, I noticed that the answering machine was blinking. The message said, "Yo motherfucker, you want to come to my neighborhood with a bunch of people looking for me? I'm going to fucking kill you when I see you." After recognizing the voice on the answering machine as one of the brothers who ran the drug business where I had worked, I became infuriated. I was ready to kill the brothers and anyone else who tried to stop me. I made sure both of my guns were loaded and I had Jenny drive me around looking for these guys. I went by all of their hangouts and drug spots in the Bronx and in upper Manhattan. I finally spotted the two brothers and their point man walking in front of the Associated Supermarket on Kingsbridge Road.

"Stop the fucking car Jenny!" I yelled at her as I prepared to exit the vehicle and execute all three of these guys in broad daylight.

"Louie, please don't do this," she cried uncontrollably. "It's not worth it. Think about Ashley. Think about your mother. They need you."

"Nah, fuck that. These motherfuckers need to die. They're threatening us and our family—why should I let them live?"

"It's not about them Louie. Why are you going to throw away the rest of your life for these guys? Please don't do it."

Somehow she managed to reach me in that moment. I could've killed those motherfuckers and they would have never seen it coming. I had walked this road before and I had to fight the urge to make things right in my twisted way of thinking.

"We'll just leave the block" Jenny continued. "Don't let them ruin your fucking life. Please, let's just leave now."

Without saying a word I motioned to Jenny to drive off but it took everything inside of me not to jump out of that car.

I had chosen to let them live and I was in a kill or be killed situation. It was a race against the clock to clear out of the neighborhood. In the two days that followed, I called all my boys, rented a U-haul truck, and packed my apartment up while people stood by with guns, ready to defend me. When the brothers saw how many soldiers I had standing guard they steered clear of us. I guess they figured they'd won the battle by pushing me off the block, but in actuality, I did what very few people are ever able to find the strength to do—I walked away. In the hood we're taught from birth that we're soft if we walk away from conflict, but as I grew into a man, I realized it was much harder to leave than to stay and fight. You always feel that hit on your pride when you decide not to show the other person how tough you really are, and that inner-city mentality has wreaked havoc on our society as a whole.

In early 1994, my stepfather Jenario Rodriguez passed away. Jenario had been in my life since the 70s and although he never became a father to me, he had become something much more important. He was the man who took care of my mother and brought her the happiness she deserved. Jenario never tried to force a father-son relationship with me, and was intelligent enough to know that treating my mother well was enough for him to earn my respect.

He lived to be in his mid 80s, and died after complications during intestinal surgery. He came out of the surgery in such a state that my mother was forced to place him in a nursing home. I remember going to shave him, wash him up, and talk to him about the latest boxing news. It was difficult for me to see a human being living in an almost vegetative state, but it taught me that we sometimes have to look death in the eye to appreciate life. The day he passed away they called Rico and me to come claim the body. I remember crying like I'd never cried before. It seemed all the tears I didn't shed for my own father were coming out in droves for him.

I spent a few nights in my mother's house making sure she'd be okay. While I was with her, she asked me, "Why don't you come stay here? I know you're not happy. Why are you putting yourself through that pain Albertico?" That's what my mother called me since birth; she never called me Luis. "You can come live with me and get yourself together."

I took heed of her words. I'd be able to help her through her grieving, and maybe in the process I'd find a bit of peace. I was the empty shell of the man I once was, and far from the man I wanted to be. While I was washing my face one day, I looked in the mirror and I saw a scary person looking back at me. I was a drug addict, an alcohol abuser, a man with no direction or purpose. I'd somehow managed to turn into the shadow of my father.

Watching Jenario's life end made me realize I wasn't guaranteed tomorrow.

It was time for me to end my unhealthy relationship with Jenny, so I packed my personal belongings and left her everything, even the car. I said goodbye to her one final time and moved in with my mother. My mother even suggested we bring Ashley to live with us as Jenny was still abusing drugs. As far as everyone was concerned Ashley was my biological child, she was the baby girl I'd raised since birth, and she was always my mother's granddaughter no matter what. I was surprised by how easily Jenny agreed to allow Ashley to come live with us. My little girl brought so much joy to my mother's life at a time when she needed it most, that I was thankful for being able to have her.

If I was ever going to get my life back on track, I was going to have to get a job. While looking through the classifieds, I saw an opening for a chef at the Graham Windham Childcare Center in Harlem. Even though I was still fucked up at the time, I managed to convince them in the interview that I was the right guy for the job. It felt good to be going back into the working world and to find that stability again.

Having Ashley and my mother in my life provided me with the clarity I'd lost so many years earlier. I never realized how much I had missed my mother until I was with her again. She had such a great sense of humor and she was a wonderful cook. She was legendary for her bread pudding and rice pudding, not to mention the Sunday dinners, which included her famous *potage y rabo encendido* (split pea soup with oxtail) it bought back the few good childhood memories I had. I got my love for cooking from mom and my grandmother Virginia, who I remember seeing when I was a little boy, dicing fresh garlic, onions, and herbs all the time. The smell of that combination always reminds me of her.

I loved every minute of being around her and enjoying life again while rebuilding that bond a son has with his mother. I even tried rebuilding a bond with my brother. One of my passions was going to Yankee Stadium and my brother was a die-hard Mets fan. Rico and I always had this love/hate relationship, (Cain & Abel), but we would try to do things together like catch Jets football games, shoot pool at Fieldston Billiards, watch championship boxing matches, and so on.

Throughout most of the 80s and early 90s the Yankees were mostly in last place and you could go to the stadium and see a few thousand people in attendance. I would get free field seat tickets, overlooking the Yankees dugout, from members of the Union League Club, sometimes as many as four or six tickets. Nobody wanted to go to Yankee stadium. It was all about the amazing Mets. Well my brother, who is six feet, five inches tall, would go with me to games all decked out in his Mets gear so he could scream shit at the Yankee players as they walked out of the dugout.

I remember one day the Yankees blew a huge six-run lead to the Cleveland Indians, and my brother stood up and screamed, "You suck!" at the players as they walked off the field. I said, "Oh fuck here we go," as he got into a vicious staring contest with Dave Winfield and Billy Martin.

It was Friday the 13th when we first met—October 13, 1995, to be exact. I was attending a staff development day at Manhattan Borough Community College, as Graham Windham employees were brought together to attend various workshops related to child services. I decided to sign up for the first workshop of the day, a storytelling class. A few minutes into the class, the most beautiful woman I'd ever laid eyes on entered the room. I was completely mesmerized and I found myself staring at the back of her head. She'd later tell me she turned around because she felt someone staring at her, but the truth was, the moment I looked into her eyes I knew it was over for me.

We found ourselves paired up with a few other students for our first exercise. We all introduced ourselves. Her name was Lizette, a fitting name for such a gorgeous woman. I was more into her than I was into her storytelling and I went gaga over every word that flowed from her pouty lips. I was trying to make her laugh as much as possible. It seemed to be working. When we were getting ready to break for recess, I asked her "Are you going to lunch?"

She replied, "Yeah."

"Where's a good place to eat around here?"

She mentioned a few places and I interrupted her with my most famous line to date: "I'm with you!"

Somehow we ended up in McDonalds, of all places. We chatted on line as we waited to place our order, and to this day Lizette will say I was rude for not offering to pay for her food. When she got her food, she walked away and tried to go hide in a two-seater thinking I wouldn't join her. When I found her, she thought, "This guy has nerve to be sitting next to me after he didn't pay for my three-dollar fish sandwich." I guess she was just used to being spoiled by men, but I was a different breed altogether.

As we spoke, we began to fall into a deep conversation about what our backgrounds were and she told me she was Cuban, to which I replied, "I'm Cuban also." It was a good look for me since she'd never dated a Cuban guy, especially one from the Boogie Down Bronx. I continued to use my humor to get her to open up, as well as to rid myself of nervous feelings. After an hour of talking I felt like we had a strong connection and I allowed myself to think there might be something worth exploring further. I didn't see Lizette for the rest of the day, until the recital at the end. As the day wrapped up I continued to make eye contact with her from a distance, and when I saw her turn to leave, I left everyone I was with to pursue her. I couldn't believe she was just going to walk away without us exchanging numbers.

"You leaving?" I asked.

"No, I'm staying. Of course I'm leaving," she said in a sarcastic tone.

"Where you going now?"

"I'm going to my car."

"Let me walk you to your car then."

"No, it's okay, my car is really, really far away."

"I don't care how far your car is, I'll walk you," I said as I reached for her briefcase.

Here she was, thinking I was cheap, but she wasn't lying about parking 20 blocks away to save ten dollars on parking. I'd come to find out later she was a silver spoon-fed Upper East Side girl. Her mother's early modeling career had opened the door to many lucrative businesses, and she was born and raised into a life of privilege complete with an Ivy League education.

By the time we reached her car, I had convinced her to go to dinner with me. I made sure to keep her laughing the entire walk and pulled out all my game to impress her—but I'd find out later that I secured my second strike because I didn't offer to pay for her parking.

"So where do you want to go to dinner?" I asked.

"Do you like seafood?" she asked.

"Yeah, of course."

"South Street Seaport is around the corner."

I guess it was her way of making me pay for the McDonalds and parking. We had a beautiful view of the water and the conversation went from deeply profound to deeply humorous. At one point during dinner I reached across her plate to clean her shrimps of the shell. As I taught her the proper techniques I also began to hand feed her and take things to a more seductive level, which definitely made an impression on her.

As the night came to a close, she offered to drive me to the 59th Street train station. I couldn't believe it, but she tried hard not to give me her number; still

I wasn't going to get out of the car without getting her number and I hoped she wouldn't give me a fake. She told me she didn't have a pen so I stood on Lexington Avenue like an idiot asking everyone who walked by for a pen. Thankfully this guy gave me one and as she drove off, she screamed, "717-1610."

As I rode the train back to the Bronx there was a definite air of excitement in my life. I had just met someone I felt could challenge me, and I was ready to do whatever it took to take things to the next level. There are the rules of dating, like waiting several days to call so that you don't appear desperate, but the next morning I called her at 8:00 am and asked her to come out with me.

"Who is this? Are you crazy? What time is it?" she asked.

"It's me Luis, from last night." I replied. "Would you like to get together today?"

"Oh sorry, but I have to work today."

"I'm not taking no for an answer. I'll show up at your house if I have to." After keeping her on the phone and making her laugh, she invited me to go see her little brother Michael play football in Queens the following day and I told her I'd bring my daughter. We went for breakfast at IHOP with her mother and brother and it was surreal. At one moment in the midst of all the laughter, I noticed we all looked like one big happy family. After eating, she told me she'd only be able to stay at her brother's game for a little while because she had to go to work, as she was holding down a second job at Kennedy Airport, working for American Airlines. She told me her mother, Gilda, would drive me back to the train station after the game.

Gilda told me she'd drop me off at the train station after she took care of a few things for a dinner party she was preparing for family that night. As I watched her run around the apartment like a crazy woman trying to clean and prepare everything I asked, "Can I help you with something?"

"I could use your help but I don't really know where to start," she told me.

"Well I'm a chef so why don't you let me help you prepare the meal?"

She was hesitant. "Well my daughter told me you are a chef but many people say that. I don't know if it's true."

"I've been a professional chef for a long time. I can help you out."

She told me she wanted to make *arroz con pollo*. "I'm going to trust you," she said.

I got to work and did my thing in the kitchen to prove I was worthy of her daughter, and let me tell you, it couldn't have worked out more beautifully. The heavens shined down on me that night and Gilda fell in love with me on the spot.

Even my daughter had a good time playing with Michael and eventually fell asleep peacefully on the sofa. As the night was winding down Lizette called her mother to say hello and make sure she got me off all right. She was shocked to hear her mother saying, "Oh my God you have no idea. I just had the best meal cooked for me and the family."

Lizette asked, "Who cooked the meal? You cooked the meal?"

"No, Luis cooked for us."

"That guy is still there? What are you talking about?"

"He's an excellent cook. We saved you some food. You need to come over and eat."

"But what happened? You were supposed to drop him off at the train a long-time ago."

"I got into some trouble and Luis helped me out. He's the best thing ever. You have to marry this guy. Now come on over."

When Lizette got to the apartment she sat down and had a meal. "This is amazing," she agreed. "Thank you so much for doing this for my mother. It's late. I'm going to drive you and Ashley home to the Bronx."

"That's cool," I told her. "I really want you to meet my mother."

We arrived home after midnight and my mother came out to greet Lizette and told her how beautiful she was. "You have to marry my son," she said in a serious tone. It was a beautiful way to end the night. We had both met the respective mothers and I was beginning to believe that this was going to turn into something special.

After that night, we began to date seriously. Due to our tough schedules we spent a lot of time on the phone. Lizette was the only woman I'd ever been able to spend hours and hours with, just laughing and talking. I was falling in love with her and one night she realized she felt the same way. She was doing her rollers when I called her; she grabbed the phone and forgot to finish setting her hair. After the hour long phone call, she had to wash and redo her hair; it was in that moment she knew she was in love.

While things with the relationship were going well, I still hadn't been able to get rid of my old bad habits, the drugs and alcohol. I was so afraid to have something good in my life that unconsciously I tried to ruin it before it got too deep. Lizette realized how bad the problem was and was tough enough to fight me over it. Over the next couple of months she stood by me and we grew even closer as we faced Jenny, who had heard about my new girl and was threatening to take Ashley away if I didn't stop dating "the stuck-up rich bitch."

As Thanksgiving rolled around, Lizette and I convinced my mother to come out to Queens as a guest at Gilda's house. Little did we know that our mothers had begun conspiring on the phone about how they were going to get us married. It was nice to get my mom out of the house because it was so rare for her to ever go out. Little did I know Lizette was speaking to my mother on a frequent basis about the problems we were having and my mother gave her advice like, "Stay with my son. It's going to take a woman like you to save him. He needs you."

After Thanksgiving, my mother began to come out of her shell. She told me she wanted to eat good seafood and I asked her if she wanted to go to City Island.

"Yes, I haven't been there in such a long time. That would be wonderful," she said with a smile on her face. We set the night. Lizette picked up my mother, Ashley, and me. We went out to Tito Puente's restaurant on the island and had another wonderful evening together. It was December and the air was cold, but the bond of family kept us warm. Things finally seemed to be looking up for me, and I was happy to have a woman I loved and wanted to spend my life with.

Lizette became my rock. She was that strong I'm-not-going-to-take-your-shit woman that I needed more than she could have possibly known. If I was supposed to meet her and didn't show up, she'd hunt me down and drag me out of whatever fucked up shit I was getting into. I can't recall how many times she found my drugs and flushed them down the toilet. She broke my bottles of alcohol and would literally shake me and yell "What are you running from?" But her most daunting words were, "Take the pain, Luis, take the pain! You need to be a man and deal with your problems."

Lizette had spent years studying everything from Buddhism to Deepak Chopra. One of her favorite authors and spiritual mentors was Marianne Williamson. She would attend monthly seminars at Town Hall with Marianne and one night she dragged me there. I can't remember exactly what Marianne Williamson said, since I was in the midst of a coke binge, but something happened to me in that room, amongst thousands of people, and I realized I had to change my life once and for all. I finally realized that I was living but I was not alive.

On December 31, 1995, my brother called me early in the morning and told me that my mother had been rushed to the hospital after suffering from severe stomach pains. When I arrived at the hospital I learned that my mother had experienced a stroke, and that the situation was very grave. The doctor came out to talk to my brother and me, and said, "I'm sorry, but your mother is not going to come out of this. We have your mother comfortably medicated but she's too deeply gone to come back. We expect her to expire in the next 24 hours."

There was nothing we could to do but pray for her soul. I made phone call after phone call to let Lizette and other family members know what was going on. By the evening, our family and friends had taken over the entire wing of the hospital. New Year came and went and our bedside vigil for my mother surely did not resemble the celebration taking place in Times Square. At one point, my mother did awaken and I was right there to talk to her. I tried to be light hearted and to make her laugh. I made peace with my mother at that the moment. As I stroked her hair and held her hand, I told her we were going to get out of there and take her to dinner again. "Mom, we'll go back to City Island." Each word was harder than the last.

How does a son say goodbye to his mother?

I spent every second of my mother's last hours telling her how much she meant to me and how grateful I was to her for being the woman she was. She made my life worth living in my darkest times and I wasn't sure how I was going to be able to survive without her in my life. I was so grateful that I'd been given the opportunity to move in with her and spend those last days with her and Ashley. Those last months became the memories I'd carry in my heart for a lifetime.

Watching her nod, smile, and laugh in her last moments, through the tubes, helped me understand that she knew she wasn't leaving this earth alone. We were by her side when my mother, Anna Cira Garcia Cedeño, drew her last breath at 3:01pm, New Year's Day, 1996. She had finally escaped the lifetime of suffering that had plagued her since birth, and as much as it hurt me, I convinced myself that she was at peace, in a better place. They say that when you're born you cry and the world is happy, and when you die the world cries and you're happy.

Two days after my mother's death, my brother showed his true colors. My mother wasn't even buried and he had people bidding for the refrigerator, the stove, the furniture, and anything else he felt he had the right to sell. Then he told me I had to be out of the apartment by the end of the month.

"I have no place to live," I said.

"I don't care. That's not my problem. You have to get out of the apartment," he said coldly. He showed me right then and there that he had the heart of our father. I was left speechless and defeated, but I calmly walked away thinking if I never saw this motherfucker again, it would be too soon. It was at that moment that my brother became dead to me, no different than my mother was. I was truly left with no family and nowhere to turn.

When I broke the news to Lizette, she said, "Marry me and come live with me. I love you."

I'd never been married before and we had only been together for three months, and a crazy three months at that. I loved Lizette, but I wasn't sure this was the right way to go about things. Was I marrying her because I had no place to live? Was I marrying her because I loved her? Or, was I going to marry her because I had no other choices in life?

The one thing I knew to be true was that I loved Lizette, so I decided to marry her, unaware that it would turn out to be the best decision I'd ever make in my lifetime. On January 12, 1996, 11 days after my mother passed away, we became husband and wife. I believe my mother watched us from the heavens as her wish came true. I had gained a new family just as abruptly as I had lost my old one. With a great woman in my corner, it was time for me to step up to the plate and become a man. I could no longer run scared and be defeated.

Track 10: That's The Scene

It was the coldest January Miami Beach had seen in over 40 years. We'd packed flip-flops and shorts, and ended up freezing our asses off every time we tried to step foot outside the hotel room, onto the oceanfront. But it wasn't all bad, as the weather allowed us to do what honeymooners do best, and we spent those three days cuddled up in the hotel room enjoying each others company. I felt blessed to have married such a wonderful woman and believed I had been granted a positive lease on life.

At Lizette's urging, I called my family in Miami and told them we were in town. They had flown in for my mother's funeral, and we had all shown that with age we were mature enough to rediscover why we called each other family.

Once they were done lecturing me for not calling sooner, they came straight to the hotel and insisted we stay with them. They paid for our three-day stay without our knowledge, then whisked us off to their mansion, which, with the tennis courts and pool, made the Holiday Inn that we just left look like the ghetto. They took us all around Miami and to great restaurants for dinner. I was still impressed by the level of success they had attained, and they showed us nothing but love and respect. We truly enjoyed every moment we spent with them. I learned to forgive and forget all that had gone wrong in the past and believe the familial reconciliation was my mother's way of introducing me to the better days that lay ahead.

When we returned to New York I was refreshed and renewed. Not only did I have a new lease on life, I had a new address. Ashley and I moved in to Lizette's studio apartment in the Upper East Side, on East 64th Street between York and First Avenue. For Ashley and me, moving to such a prestigious location was nothing short of a culture shock. For a while it seemed that life could not get any better.

Soon I would find out that I would not be allowed to bring along an old friend into my new posh environment. Lizette had found my strong box, which had my Sig Sauer 9mm handgun and an assortment of bullets, and told me that under no condition would I ever need a weapon; she assured me that I was now safe. We took a walk in the middle of the night and threw the gun and bullets into the East River. Coincidentally, I had taken to power walking by the East River from 63rd street to 125th Street, and back, almost every day, and had shed 65 lbs. in a few months. All the mental and spiritual preparation had now inspired me to make a physical transformation, and let's just say I left a lot baggage by that river.

One afternoon while reflecting on all the positive changes in my life, I decided to get a new tattoo. I wanted something meaningful that would remind me of who

I once was and of who I was now becoming so I got a five-by-five inch tattoo on my right thigh of the Chinese character for "forever." With this I vowed to never do drugs, drink excessively, be violent towards others, or return to prison, but more importantly I promised that I would truly love myself forever.

Working with the kids at the Graham Windham in Harlem taught me how to give freely of myself. When you give something of your heart without expecting anything in return, that's when you receive it back tenfold. When I first began working at the center, I realized that everything they were feeding these kids was unhealthy, prepackaged and processed, and tasted terrible. I immediately set out to make the food healthier and tastier, preparing fresh meals from scratch. It was important to me that these youth be fed according to humanity's standards and not their parents' social and economic standing. I also began to mentor the kids in the culinary arts. I made it my personal mission to help these kids believe in themselves the way I wished someone would have believed in me.

I also volunteered at the Momentum Project, which fed people suffering from AIDS, and the homeless. These were all things I began to implement of my own free will, and believe me when I tell you, it gave me a great deal of satisfaction giving back to the community.

★ ★ ★ ★ ★

One afternoon in February 1997, my boss called me into her office, and I could tell by the look on her face that something was up. "Luis you know that we love you around here. You do a great job and we'd love to keep you on, but we just found out you weren't honest on your resume," she said.

Surprised, I asked, "What do you mean?"

"Well, you said you'd never been arrested for a felony, and your record check came back that you'd been arrested in your past for a violent crime."

"Yes, it's true. I was arrested almost 20 years ago for a mistake I made when I was a teenager. I didn't think I had to report it because I was told I was pardoned and received an early release from parole."

Shit, I knew only governors pardoned people but I played the story up hoping she'd show some sympathy in her decision. I knew that if I didn't lie on the application, I never would have landed the job, but that explanation wasn't going to get me anywhere.

My boss explained that she'd see what she could do. She got back to me a few days later. "Luis, we're going to let you stay on because you are such a great worker, but please don't make us regret the decision."

I was called back to the office a second time, on a cold February morning in 1997. This time the receptionist asked, "Do you have an older daughter?"

What would make her ask me that question, I thought to myself. "Yeah, I do."

"Well she called here looking for you," she said with a straight face.

"Come on. Stop bullshitting me."

"A young lady called here for you and said she is your daughter."

"What's her name?" I asked calmly.

When she said Tammy, I must have turned five shades of red. I couldn't imagine how she found me, or even why she came looking for me. When she handed me the phone number all I could say was, "Holy shit."

I immediately called Tammy and in my excitement I didn't even get the chance to ask her how she found me. After making a lot of small talk, she told me she was in her second year at New York University, which blew me away; my daughter was attending NYU.

As Lizette and I traveled to see her that evening, I thought about how timing was everything. How if my daughter came looking for me one year earlier she would've found a miserable, drug and alcohol dependent, shell of a man. I couldn't have appreciated more that she'd found me at this time in my life, when things were good for me. After 15 years of not seeing my baby girl, not knowing how and who she was, a nervous anticipation almost paralyzed me. Tammy wasn't a little girl anymore, and when I first laid eyes on her, I couldn't believe the beautiful woman she had become.

When we sat down to speak, the conversation turned to years past. She told me how her mother had left her to be raised by her grandmother, who told Tammy on several occasions that I didn't want to be a part of her life. I just shook my head as tears welled up in my eyes. How was I to explain to her that nothing could be further from the truth, while at the same time not going against the woman who had raised her?

"You know Tammy, one day I'll give you the full story of what happened when you were a baby. But please believe me when I tell you I tried my very best to be a part of your life for many years. I am so happy that you found me."

Much later I would find out I had my brother Ricardo, of all people, to thank for this happy reunion. Apparently while he was moonlighting as a security guard in a store in White Plains she walked up to him and asked him, "Do you have a brother named Luis Cedeño?" He told her yes and when she introduced herself, he grabbed her with the biggest bear hug ever. She remembered him from when she was a very young girl and visited my mother's house while I was in prison. She later told me she remembered how tall he was, and his ever-present smile and glasses; she just knew it was him. That day he gave her all my contact information. I could not believe that out of all the stores in the world, my daughter would walk into that one. My life would never be the same again.

The timing was fortuitous. The previous year Lizette and I had to give Ashley back to Jenny after she started to threaten us with a custody battle. Although I knew Ashley was better off living with us, Jenny reminded me that Ashley wasn't my biological daughter. Against our wishes, we returned Ashley to her and eventually would never see either of them again. I lost one daughter and the universe gave me back the other.

I never felt the need to tell Tammy about my difficult life. When we met, all she knew was that I had a good job, a wonderful wife, a nice place to live, and I was traveling the world. I've never heard more beautiful words than the day Tammy said, "Dad, I'm very proud of you." It made me understand that everything I'd ever done led me to this moment. I could finally begin to be proud of myself and find closure.

Fate continued to reconnect me to my past when, a few weeks later, I was listening to Kiss FM on the kitchen radio. The host Fred Buggs said that he'd be right back with special guests, the Cold Crush Brothers, and I just about lost my fucking mind. The last time I'd seen Caz was in 1987. He'd shown up at my apartment on Parkview Terrace in the Bronx. The conversation was deep, but awkward; it felt as though we were unable to find the bond that once allowed us to call each other brothers. Maybe too much time had passed or maybe we'd just grown too far apart to feel the same friendship we once felt for one another, but either way, it was a low note to end on for our tight brotherhood.

When Bugsy came on the radio he said, "We have the legendary Cold Crush Brothers in the house. JDL, Tony Tone, Grandmaster Caz, Easy AD, Kay Gee, and Charlie Chase."

I was jumping up and down in the kitchen saying, "Yo those are my boys!" while the other people in the kitchen looked at me like I was crazy. I didn't tell anyone—not even Lizette—that I was the first Latino Hip Hop DJ to rock the turntables, and they damn sure didn't know about my history with my partner Grandmaster Caz. It's just not something I walked around talking about. To tell you the truth it just didn't seem important at the time. I was Luis the chef. It wasn't until many years later that I began to grasp the importance of my roll in the emergence of Hip Hop, especially amongst Latinos.

You see I wanted people to respect me, appreciate me, and love me. Who the fuck was going to respect me if I was sniffing coke and drinking with them, talking about, "Yeah, I'm DJ Disco Wiz, Hip Hop's first Latino DJ?" They would've thought I was a bumbling fool and clowned me, rightfully so. So if I was ever going to make a comeback, I was going to do it when I was in a good place. If I was going to call myself a pioneer, I was going to do it with honor. I had no intentions of coming back as a jaded pioneer looking for a handout and reparations. I didn't need forty acres and a mule. I wanted to continue to earn my stripes the same way I did all those years earlier when I was helping trail blaze this shit with my brother Casanova Fly. I would bring people into my world in a way that they'd walk away saying, "That's why I love Hip Hop."

Hearing Caz on the radio made me realize what I'd been missing all those years, and at that very moment, Lizette called me on the phone. I told her, "My friends are on the radio!"

"What friends?"

"These guys I used to roll with back in the days, Cold Crush and Grandmaster Caz."

"Really? You know those guys? What radio station are they on?"

"They're on Kiss FM."

"I used to work at Kiss," she said.

"Yeah, they're on right now with Bugsy."

I knew my wife was in the music industry prior to us meeting, but I was a little surprised when she said, "I have Bugsy's house number. You want to see your friends?"

"Are you fucking kidding me?"

"If you want to see your friends I'll hook it up right now. I'll call you right back." Shit, who would have thought that my wife would be my link back into Hip Hop?

Lizette later told me that she called the house and spoke with Bugsy's wife who gave her his direct number. Once she got Bugsy on the phone she told him who I was and they couldn't believe it. She got the address to the studio, and soon enough I was on my way to meet face-to-face with my peoples from the past.

I left work early and hopped on the train to go downtown. When I got to Kiss FM I asked for a piece of paper and a pen and wrote *This is DJ Disco Wiz*. "Can you give this to any member of the Cold Crush Brothers?" I asked.

As soon as someone read the note I heard a lot of rumbling and "Oh shits!" and the studio door was kicked open. All of the Cold Crush Brothers, along with members of the group K7, came rushing out. Red Alert and Chris Mercado, who had worked with Lizette, also came out to give me a hug. It had been ten years since I'd seen these brothers and being reunited with Caz was truly amazing. I'm sure he never knew the hard road I had traveled up to this point, but I did know that all those years that I was away, I was with him in spirit. Caz has always been my portal to the Hip Hop movement, and I loved and respected him for keeping my name alive in the game for over 30 years.

As I began traveling, and attending various Hip Hop events, it seemed like I never left. I gradually started contributing to the culture: giving interviews, judging DJ competitions, and making my comeback into Hip Hop.

Charlie Chase and I had been good friends in the mid 70s. I knew him back when he was with a Latino collective called Tom & Jerry, which was a salsa and disco DJ group. I recall Charlie wanting to play Hip Hop back then, but since it wasn't his sound system, he didn't have the say in what got played. He used to come through and check out Caz and I all the time, and I guess he was getting in his Hip Hop fix through us. Once I was locked up he picked up the baton for Latinos and ran with it, and In the words of Forrest Gump, "That's all I have to say about that."

In 1998, I called an old colleague who was now in a management position at the Union League Club, and he referred me to Jean-Yves Piquet, formerly the chef at Le Cygne, considered by many to be among the finest French restaurants in New York. Jean-Yves was now the Executive Chef at the University Club. At my interview, I was hired on the spot, and I was back amongst the elite again, working in the culinary capital of the world, on Fifth Avenue.

I began working extremely hard to meet the standards of one of the finest, most prestigious places in the world. The money was great, and Lizette and I began traveling quite a bit, enjoying life the way it was meant to be lived. We started by traveling to most of the islands in the Caribbean, and we even took Tammy with us to Puerto Rico for a week.

Lizette told me she always wanted to be a teacher. She said she'd thought about it many times and was now ready to pursue her dream. Lizette had graduated from

Fordham University and held a double degree in Psychology and Child Development. She had even gone to live and study in Rome, as an exchange student in her senior year, for six months. She was immediately hired to teach high school Spanish and Italian at Mount St. Michael Academy in Mount Vernon, New York. The only real sacrifice we made was her taking a nearly 30 thousand-dollar salary cut, but it was the best decision she ever made. We now had more time to be together especially during the summers. Life was good and we continued to work hard and play harder.

Living in the Upper East Side of Manhattan can really spoil a guy. I immediately acquired a taste for the finer things in life. Lizette and I enjoyed everything New York had to offer; we spent evenings at Broadway shows and weekends at the Metropolitan Museum of Art, and on walks through Central Park. We would rarely miss a mass at Unity Church near Lincoln Center, followed by brunch with friends and her family. I quickly found out that this was how one should live, and somehow I fit right in.

Lizette and I especially loved to go away on weekends to the Poconos, in Pennsylvania. For a couple of city slickers such as ourselves driving up into the mountains proved to be the escape we always craved. In the winters we would ski and in the summers we would relax by the lakes. We ended up falling in love with the area so much that we began house shopping. All of the hard work Lizette and I had put in was finally going to pay us back with something tangible. We found a nice piece of land in Mt. Pocono and decided to build the house of our dreams—and what a dream it was.

It was Memorial Day weekend. Lizette and I were preparing to head up to the Poconos to check on the progress of our future home. I'll never forget that morning. I was shaving to get ready for our trip. As I dragged the razor over my neck I noticed a lump in my throat. I've always been very conscious of my body and I would've noticed the lump had it been there previously. When I ran my finger over the lump it felt like someone was making a knuckle inside my neck. It was rock hard, but not painful, and as I gulped I realized something was seriously wrong.

As I starred at myself in the mirror, the darkest cloud I'd ever known came over me and stripped me of all the feeling in my body. There are some things in this life you just immediately know, a feeling that leaves no room for mistakes.

My heart sunk. A million thoughts flooded my head. Right when everything in my life was going great, cancer came knocking on my door.

Motherfucking cancer…

The scene was being set for the hardest fought war I'd ever have to wage. I had an enemy in my body, a true killer, and I wasn't sure I'd be victorious in the end. I could feel death calling me like it never had before. It was getting louder, and there was nothing I could do to drown it out.

All I could do was brace for the rough roads ahead. I put the razor down and screamed for the only comfort in the world I had ever known, "Lizette…"

Track 11: We Had Fun

The trip to our dream house was replaced with a trip to the doctor's office. After a complete checkup the doctor gave me a clean bill of health and told me the lump in my throat was nothing more than an inflamed lymph node. He put me on antibiotics for ten days to fight the infection and sent me on my merry way, but something didn't sit right. I knew my body well enough to know that this lump wasn't a result of an infection, but all I could do was take the antibiotics and hope for the best.

After a few weeks the lump was still there. The doctor sent me for a CAT scan and an ultrasound where specialists discovered the lump was a solid mass; they performed a biopsy while I waited on pins and needles for the results to come back. The cancer was confirmed, and though I was not surprised by the results, I felt defeated.

It was June 1999. Lizette and I went to New York Hospital, where I had the entire lump removed and sent to the lab for analysis. After several days of pacing I was informed that the lump tested positive for thyroid cancer. Again, there was no real surprise. Lizette was standing by my side as we set out in search of a good surgeon to help and guide me through the fight of my life. I went to a team of top doctors that included Dr. Robert Gelfand and Dr. Harry Gruenspan, both of New York Presbyterian Hospital, and Dr. Norris K. Lee, one of the best surgeons in New York Hospital. Although I had lost several family members to this deadly disease, I was fortunate to have good health insurance, allowing me the best care possible.

I had no idea what to expect but I had a million questions. Lizette, ever the hammer, grilled Dr. Lee relentlessly as he explained the procedure to us. I would undergo a radical, or total, thyroidectomy. The doctors were going to cut my neck from one side to the other; in the Bronx, they called this a Columbian necktie and not too many people survived an incision like this. In the surgery, I would lose some of my parathyroid glands, the glands that provide calcium, and Dr. Lee would also be separating my trachea from the thyroid gland. Even though I wasn't one of those DJs who liked to scream on the microphone, I'd still need my voice in the future to shout, "Yes yes y'all!"

The survival rate of people with thyroid cancer was in the 90th percentile, which provided me with some relief. As I prepared for surgery, I made sure I put my affairs in order. Being in my mid-thirties, newly married, and enjoying life, I never stopped to think about what kind of financial burden I'd put on my wife if I were to die. Getting cancer made me realize that as a married man and father, I needed to be responsible, even in death. I wrote my will, took out life insurance, and I made sure to tell Lizette to bury me in the Bronx. Even though I saw some of the hardest times in my life in the borough, I also laughed and loved hard in the Boogie Down Bronx. It would be my first and last home.

The very night before my surgery, I went to a Cold Crush Brothers anniversary concert at S.O.B.'s in lower Manhattan. When Caz called me on stage to tell me how much I meant to him and Hip Hop, it took everything I had not to breakdown in tears. I looked out into the crowd, took a deep breath, and allowed myself to feel good. That night gave me a sense of closure. If I were to leave this earth the next day, I would be leaving after being reunited with my daughter, stepping on stage with the Cold Crush Brothers one last time, and having Lizette by my side. I couldn't have asked for more than that.

As they prepared to wheel me into surgery the following day, I could see the sullen expressions on everyone's faces. To be honest, I was scared shitless, but I never showed it. Always one to crack a joke in times of difficulty, I said, "Make sure you have lunch ready for me when I get back. I'm gonna be hungry."

Lizette cracked a smile, and I said, "Don't worry baby. A little tuck here, a little tuck there—I'll probably look better without the double chin! Maybe they'll even give me a little lipo while I'm under, make some improvements." As they wheeled me away the last thing I said to her was, "I love you. Don't worry, I'll be right back."

I would learn a few days later that I didn't do too well on the operating table. The standard three-hour surgery turned into a nine-hour ordeal due to serious complications during the surgery. I can't say that I saw my life flash before me or heard voices calling me, but I do know that I made Dr. Lee earn his pay that day.

When I came to in recovery, I saw Lizette, who laughed and told me I looked like Frankenstein all stapled up (but after she left the room she broke down in tears). I had survived the toughest battle of my life but the road back would prove to be grueling as complications from surgery landed me in the Intensive Care Unit.

I developed a disease called Ménière's, brought on by excessive fluid in the ears, causing recurring episodes of vertigo. For someone like me, who was never sickly, having these sensations of abnormal movement and dizziness left me feeling like I was going to die. It took me six months to finally get back to work, but I would never be the same again. I was now a cancer survivor who depended on various medications everyday just to live, and with the post surgical complications of weight gain; loss of energy, desire, and drive; plus high blood pressure and high cholesterol, I could no longer keep up the demanding pace of being a chef at a high-end establishment.

It was Lizette's love and support that gave me the strength to survive. If there's such a thing as getting cancer at the right time, I guess you can say it couldn't have happened at a better time. Having learned every lesson the hardest way possible, I was determined to live my life to the fullest. Nothing was going to stop me from chasing my dreams, both past and present. As the saying goes, with all dark storms eventually comes light.

I had met Carlito Rodriguez, then Editor in Chief of the Bible of Hip Hop, *The Source*. As a Latino in a position of power, he was looking to shine a light on other Latinos who had been an integral part of the movement from its earliest days. We became fast friends on the phone and even met a few times at his office in Union Square. One time I brought down my collection of early Hip Hop flyers, and got a kick out of watching the young staff bug out over them. Soon afterwards, Carlito told me he wanted to include me on a retrospective piece for the Millennium edition and I was honored to be remembered after so many years. When the January 2000 issue dropped, I sat down to read Carlito's words in the magazine. In a piece titled, "El Mero Mero," he wrote:

The mid-70s. Almost five years before it is to be heard on the radio, Hip Hop music slowly spreads through neighborhoods in the Bronx. In one area, around 183rd and Creston Avenue, a young Cuban-Puerto Rican DJ with a love for the music and culture follows the lead of his partner and longtime friend, Casanova Fly (a.k.a. Grandmaster Caz), establishing his rep by doing free parties in the park and rockin' neighborhood clubs like the Blue Lagoon. Despite heavy criticism from those who feel that Latinos have no business on the wheels of steel, the young DJ keeps his parties movin'. Although he soon after drops out of sight, no real trip through Hip Hop's memory lane would be complete without giving props to Disco Wiz, rap's first Latino DJ.

(Rodriquez, Carlito. "El Mero Mero." *The Source*, January 2000.)

Reading about myself in *The Source* and seeing my name listed as rap's first Latino DJ was all I needed at the time. It meant that I still mattered to Hip Hop after all those years and my contribution would always be respected. It was my re-introduction to Hip Hop and I wasn't looking back.

Less than a month later, Caz called me. He always made it a point to invite me to events, but I often declined as work and health reasons kept me away. This time he told me about a meeting in Harlem where some people were interviewing graffiti and Hip Hop pioneers, and I remember he had said, "Yo Lou, you should really try to be here if you can, this is big!"

Paul Allen, at the time the third richest man in the world and co-founder of Microsoft, was about to turn his private music collection into a state of the art museum—and with an estimated worth of 7.5 billion dollars in 1999, Allen could've purchased the entire borough of the Bronx and everyone in it. Allen brought in Jim Fricke, Senior Curator at the Experience Music Project in Seattle, to document the history of the culture in a series of interviews with the b-boys and girls, graffiti writers, DJs, and MCs who were there from the beginning. Being invited to speak about the part I played within the Hip Hop movement was huge for me, and I appreciated Caz taking me along for the ride.

I've always been a pack rat and to this day I don't throw shit away. If I need to find an old movie stub from the 80s, I'm sure I have one stuffed away somewhere. Lucky for me I'd kept over 100 of the original back-in-the-day flyers from the jams Disco Wiz and Casanova Fly and others used to throw in the parks and clubs. I offered to donate two of my original flyers to the museum as part of their permanent exhibit: one from the Webster P.A.L battle with Afrika Bambaataa and another flyer of the late, and rarely mentioned, Disco King Mario.

I was flown out to Seattle with Caz and the Cold Crush Brothers for the opening reception of the exhibition. It was VIP all the way. When I arrived at the venue Metallica was on stage playing "Enter Sandman." When I looked in one direction I'd see the Red Hot Chili Peppers, Eminem, and Dr. Dre. Then I'd turn my head another way and see James Brown walking by. We went backstage and met Chuck D from Public Enemy, but the highlight of my evening was chilling with Kid Rock who was just so cool and down to earth. At one point he even broke out into a freestyle with the Cold Crush. It was truly a magical event. It wasn't that I was star struck; I just felt on top of the world.

Soon after I returned home, Jim informed me that he was working on a book based on our interviews, co-written by *Wild Style* creator Charlie Ahearn, later titled *Yes Yes Y'all*. Fricke knew about my flyer collection and told me he wanted to license the rights to reproduce these images in the book, as well as have me contribute further interviews for the book. I wasn't interested in just telling the story of who DJ Disco Wiz was—I wanted all the pioneers to get proper credit and shine. I wanted the world to recognize us for our contributions to a movement that was now generating billions of dollars in revenues all over the world. Prior to the exhibition at Experience Music Project and the publication of *Yes Yes Y'all*, no one was documenting Hip Hop history. I can still remember the frustrating conversations I used to have with Jim. He would say, "Wiz, can you believe that no one wants to publish us just because we are writing a book about a bunch of guys who precede the likes of Run DMC? It is as if they have no idea, care, or ever heard of the likes of you all." That fueled something inside of me. Through my struggles I discovered that the true measure of a man is not found in money, but in love, family, and for me, Hip Hop.

One day Tammy called to tell me that she was pregnant. I couldn't believe it! I was going to be a grandfather at the age of 39. On July 29, 2000, my grandson Cameron was born into this world, and I could not have been any prouder. The birth of my grandchildren Cameron, Phoenix, Moses, and Savana has been the greatest gift in my life. Every day I spend around them is truly a blessing. Some days I just look at them in wonder and total disbelief that I could be so lucky.

And just as my daughter had her children, Lizette and I wanted a family of our own. Since our first week together, Lizette and I had talked about having a baby. Don't forget we were married after three months of meeting each other; we were all about, "Let's get married, have babies, and conquer the world!" It was all Lizette ever talked about, and I knew she wanted to be a mom more than she wanted anything else in the world. In April 2001, after five years of trying, Lizette called me at work with very exciting news. "Honey we did it! We did it!" She was yelling with excitement. "We're pregnant!" Our last wish was finally coming true.

One rainy day on her drive home from school, as Lizette stood in traffic on the FDR Drive, she was rear-ended by a woman talking on her cell phone. All Lizette really remembers was feeling the impact, the whiplash, and stepping out of the car in the middle lane of the FDR in the pouring rain. When the other driver asked her if she was all right Lizette could only reply, "Oh my God, I'm pregnant."

The next day at work, Lizette started to bleed. By the time we reached New York Hospital the doctors informed us we'd lost the baby. But that wasn't all. As we sat at her gynecologist's office following her miscarriage, Lizette told Dr. Claudia Holland, "Oh, by the way, I found this lump under my arm while I was shaving."

"How long has that been there?"

Lizette told her a few months but that she thought it was part of the pregnancy. Dr. Holland gave Lizette the name of a doctor she should go see immediately. Less than one week after we lost our child, Lizette told me she had been diagnosed with Hodgkin's disease. I must have stared at her for several minutes, trying to decipher

her words and think of a way to respond.

The only thing I could say was, "Come on man. Don't fuck around Lizette."

"Yeah papi, I have cancer," she told me.

Learning that my wife had Hodgkin's disease was by far the most difficult news I'd ever have to swallow. I never had anybody in my entire life love me the way Lizette does. Growing up the way I did taught me how not to depend on anyone for anything, but I broke all those rules when I met Lizette. She's my best friend, my life partner, my rock, my source of strength, and my every-fucking-thing. I couldn't imagine having to walk a day on this earth without her by my side.

You have no idea how much praying I did, and how much soul seeking was necessary, to find a way to wake up each day and keep moving in a positive forward direction. I needed God to save my wife's life.

God, I hope you're listening. I really need you right now to hear me. I need you to understand that I will do anything it takes to keep my wife by my side. Whatever it takes God, I got you. If it wasn't for Lizette, I wouldn't be a quarter of the man I am today. She took in a fucked up dude, a guy who was completely destroyed and had nothing to live for, and she gave me purpose. She broke this man down… a man who had been destroyed by years of physical and mental abuse and she built me back up. She used love and compassion to help me lay a foundation and she made me brick-by-brick. She made me believe in myself when I didn't believe in anything. Please hear my prayer, and if you must take someone, please take me instead of Lizette. I can't live without her and I don't want to.

I never stopped praying for her life… never.

As a child, Lizette was in poor health. She pretty much lived in Manhattan hospitals until the age of ten, and because of that, her chances of surviving the aggressive cancer were slim to none. But I couldn't allow myself to think that way; I had to believe she was going to survive this, otherwise I would've fallen apart.

When Lizette came home from her biopsy she had a huge incision underneath her underarm. It reminded me of a catcher's mitt, that's how open and large the cut was. Cleaning my wife's wound was a difficult thing for me to do. Not only was I not a doctor, but digging in there to get all the pus out with sterile gauze and gloves was something I had to do two or three times a night to keep any kind of infection from setting in.

Lizette's fight with cancer was a million times worse than mine. I didn't have to go through chemotherapy; I only experienced radiation, which isn't as bad. I didn't have to lose my hair like she did. She went through six months of treatments, and because of the aggressiveness of the cancer and her history with Sickle Cell Anemia, she had to deal with equally aggressive chemo.

Mentally, my wife is the strongest person I've ever met, but physically she'd always been a little weak. This battle she was waging with cancer was kicking her ass and I had to be there to fight every step of the way. These were some of the most difficult days of my life, but I stayed strong and did anything necessary to keep my wife from getting sicker, and to keep her comfortable.

One of the toughest things Lizette and I had to deal with during her fight was seeing her beautiful hair fall out in chunks. My wife, the gorgeous model, the most stunning woman I'd ever laid eyes on, was deteriorating, and I could tell it was tearing her apart. I made it a point to reassure my wife that I thought she was the most beautiful woman in the world and I meant every word.

Lizette fought the hair loss so hard, wanting to keep any bit of hair she could salvage since she was still teaching her last month of the school year. She didn't want to see her students crying for her or worrying about her, but eventually the bald patches on her head just didn't look right, so I told her it was time to let go of her hair and to let me cut it. It was as if I awoke a monster in my wife. She screamed, yelled, and called me every fucking name in the book, but I stood strong and firm with her and let her know it was time to let me cut it, because it just didn't look right to walk around like that.

When I sat her down and shaved her head, I tried to hold back the tears as I watched them well up in her eyes. I felt like shit, but I knew I was doing the right thing. When I was done shaving her head, she lost it for hours. She was inconsolable and there was nothing I could do to comfort for her. I thought she was screaming and crying because she hated me, but later she told me that this was the moment she finally accepted the cancer.

If things weren't bad enough, that same summer, my grandmother Virginia passed away after a long battle with breast cancer, and my cousin Junior, who had since come home from prison and cleaned up his life, was paralyzed in a car accident.

I'd spent half of my life under dark clouds but the years my wife and I battled cancer were no doubt the darkest. The storms never seemed to end and each passing day was a war with an enemy we couldn't see. But the one thing I realized was that I wasn't walking alone and I didn't have to; these were battles Lizette and I fought together. The treacherous paths we walked only led us to a powerful love that can be compared to none other I've ever known. Lizette would prove to be the true warrior I knew she was. God answered my prayers and allowed me to keep my wife.

In keeping with the tradition of Catholic schools, my wife was let go from her teaching job by the Archdiocese of New York. After five months of fighting cancer, Lizette began to gain some of her strength back after the chemo had devastated her body. We both decided it would be a good idea for her to fly out to Miami and relax with one of her good friends. She spent a week out there enjoying the sun and prepared to return home to me on Tuesday morning, September 11, 2001.

I remember while prepping for the lunch shift that morning, the dining and kitchen staff began running upstairs to the employees lounge. I said, "What the fuck is going on? Is somebody fighting?"

"NO!" they screamed back. "The World Trade Center is on fire…"

I stood in front of the TV with hundreds of employees, all of us staring confused at the images on the screen. The second plane went into the tower right before our eyes. Everybody started screaming and crying and I stood there frozen for what seemed like forever. Man, I had seen a lot of shit in my life, but I just couldn't believe this. When the towers tragically collapsed, I ran outside and stood on 54th Street and Sixth Avenue looking up at the debris and dark clouds of destruction. There were thousands of people on the street with me, all of us stunned by fear. It seemed like the end of the world.

All communications were down and I had no idea where my wife was. After eight nerve-wracking hours I finally received a call from Lizette. She was stranded in Miami and had no way of knowing when she would be coming home.

I was alone on the darkest day of the history of our country, and when Lizette returned to me, I held her tighter than I ever had before. It was then that I realized I had a life partner to walk through these perilous days with.

When Lizette decided to return to work, she landed a teaching gig in Stamford, Connecticut. But after a while the commute became too strenuous for her, so we decided to pack up and move out of the city to follow her job. It was a drastic, but positive change, and I have to tell you that living in an oceanfront home made me understand that this is the way life is meant to be lived.

We had a lot of fun in the years that followed, but nothing compared to our trip to Hawaii in 2004 for Lizette's 40th birthday. We spent two of the greatest weeks of our lives in Honolulu and Maui. I spent countless hours staring out into the Pacific Ocean thinking about all the struggles we'd survived over the years.

The day we returned home from Hawaii, we spent hours going through the stack of mail. Prior to leaving on vacation I'd had a routine blood test performed. When I saw the letter marked *URGENT* in big, red lettering from my doctor's office my heart sank into the deepest part of my soul.

An abnormality has been detected in your blood. Please contact the office immediately.

Track 12: It's Just Begun

What was the magic number? How long would it be before I was free of cancer? The doctor told me that if I survived five years without a recurrence, I would be in the clear. I had just hit that five-year mark when I opened the envelope marked *URGENT.*

Emotionally I took my second bout with cancer a lot tougher than the first, but physically I was better prepared. Once I awoke from the surgery I knew I'd be fine. I knew how to beat this shit.

The major difference this time was that Lizette was out working to support us both, so I was left alone, with my thoughts for company—and a big part of dealing, with cancer was filling my time and my mind with positive things. The first time I fought cancer I worried about seeing another day but the second time around I didn't entertain those thoughts.

Around 2004 I discovered the magic of the written word. I can't pinpoint the exact moment when I began to write everything down, but eventually it became habit. It felt good to spill my thoughts out into a journal, a napkin, or a receipt. There is something very therapeutic about the process of writing your thoughts down without worrying if they'd be read or even make any sense. With no intention other than freedom, I was discovering a love for poetry, and writing became my salvation. Having repressed so many dark memories, it wasn't until I started writing that I understood the importance of being brutally honest. I didn't really understand the power poetry had. It was a new form of expression that I discovered when I was at my sickest. I was alive but I was not among the living, and no matter how sick I was, when I found the strength to write I became alive in a way I'd never felt before. Poetry became my lifeline.

Having cancer a second time made me realize I was very angry that I had done all the things that were asked of me, and still this shit came back. Again I would be out of work, but unlike the first time, my desire to return would not be there when it was over. Something had happened to me. I took the recurrence as a sign that it was time for me to rejoin Hip Hop.

Everyone in Hip Hop is part of a billion-dollar industry where everything seems to revolve around how much money is changing hands. Your success is gauged by it; your respect is measured by it; but our history is riddled with death, destruction, and oblivion. The current state of Hip Hop was beginning to leave a real bad taste in my mouth. I couldn't have been more ashamed of what the movement had become and how global business sat back and cashed large checks at the expense of our communities. It was blood money at its best, and no one seemed to care enough to speak out against this new form of genocide taking place all around us.

I have never made any money off of Hip Hop and I don't want the almighty dollar to dictate the rules to me. Once you allow payola to determine your playlist, you've shitted on three generations of a movement, and I wasn't going to make a new name for myself shitting on anyone. I'd survived way too fucking much to make that my final legacy.

Once upon a time, Hip Hop had tried like hell to save my life, but the streets wouldn't allow it. Now it seemed the streets were out to destroy Hip Hop and I felt the need to do something about it. Hip Hop was an art form that taught me a sense of community. I remember its power and worked with those who respect its glory days. The energy of days past takes center stage at grassroots Hip Hop jams like those put on by Christie and Fabel Pabon's Tools of War series, and the Rock Steady and Zulu Nation Anniversaries, but I saw a big problem with today's artists all but forgetting who we were.

The pioneers were beginning to be stereotyped as bitter-ass old dudes who haven't left the 70s and never stopped bigging themselves up for their accomplishments of yesteryear, and in some cases these stereotypes weren't far off. If you're 48 years old and you're trying to battle a 19-year-old MC you're a clown. If you can't use the gift you were given to mentor and uplift without being narcissistic, you're not necessary to this game. As pioneers, it's our responsibility to guide and educate the next generation about why we started this movement, to expand the culture and build a better future with the resources at our disposal. We are the elder statesmen of this movement and our role is that of a historian, educator, and caretaker.

Sadly, many Hip Hop pioneers have died penniless, and that is the worst kind of disrespect a community can bestow upon its ancestors. Malcolm is gone, Martin is gone, Black Panthers and Young Lords are all gone. The movement that gave birth to Public Enemy, X-Clan, and KRS-One is gone. Just at that point in time when our voice was starting to be heard again, our streets were flooded with guns and narcotics, materialism, and a harsh realism that shifted our focus away from community and right back to that do or die mentality. It wasn't until crack spread like wildfire into our communities that the price for peddling the drug became our lives. I was part of that very problem back in the 80s and early 90s and am deeply sorry for my role. I owe my community reparations.

I realized that a lot of Latinos looked to me for guidance because of my status in the game. I heard countless stories about how Latinos felt like outcasts for so many years, that Hip Hop was a black movement and that we had no place in it, or were some Johnnies come lately. Nothing could be further from the truth. We have always been here, since day one, and have blessed every element throughout Hip Hop's evolution - b-boying, graffiti, MCing, DJing, and knowledge of self.

Through poetry I found that voice I'd been missing for so many years, and I was going to use it to cement my return to Hip Hop. My poems—"The Land Before the Rhyme", "The Product", and "Concrete Jungle"—each told a story from my struggle and I began to understand these works were an extension of Hip Hop. When I first ventured into the spoken word community I discovered that my Hip Hop resume was no free pass. No one seemed to know who I was, which made my poetry even more necessary.

The first time I performed for a large crowd was at the Nuyorican Poets Café. The Café was founded in 1973 by Miguel Algarin and co-founded by Bittman Bimbo Rivas, but it was made famous by the late Miguel Piñero. Piñero was someone I looked up to as a writer, not only because he was of Puerto Rican heritage, but because of his own survival story.

Miguel Piñero was born in Gurabo, Puerto Rico, and when he was four, immigrated with his parents to New York. His father abandoned the family in 1954 and his mother moved into a basement and lived on welfare. He received his first criminal conviction at the age of 11 and was a drug addict with a long criminal record by the time he was 20. In 1972, when Piñero was 25 years old, he was incarcerated in Sing Sing prison for second degree armed robbery. While serving time, he wrote the play *Short Eyes*, which was later presented at Riverside Church in Manhattan, in 1974. Theater impresario Joseph Papp saw the play and was so impressed that he moved the production to the Public Theater and then to Broadway, where it was nominated for six Tony Awards. In the 1970s, Piñero co-founded the Nuyorican Poets Cafe with a group of artists, including Miguel Algarín and Lucky Cienfuegos. The Café was a place for performance of poetry about the experience of being a Puerto Rican in New York. Piñero also received a Guggenheim Fellowship before he died on June 17, 1988 in New York City, from cirrhosis.

One day while coming home from a doctor's appointment, I stopped by Barnes & Noble and stumbled upon a book called —*said the shotgun to the head*, by Saul Williams, and was blown away. My new-found inspiration now had a name. It took me almost a year to write and memorize "The Land Before the Rhyme." I've seen the illest MC's spit verses, but they never moved me to the point of tears. Poets die on the stage right before your eyes, and I knew if I was going to stand amongst them that I would have to expose myself in full. I wanted the audience to feel my words as I had lived them, to leave a little piece of myself on that stage as well as in their hearts.

On August 10, 2005, just one day before my birthday, I stepped into the legendary Nuyorican, more than ready to rock the crowd. All of my family and friends including Caz came out; the place was packed to the hinges. I was nervous as fuck when they called me up to the stage. I calmed my nerves and closed my eyes as I grabbed the mic. Every word flowed perfectly together in rhythmic form because I believed in what I was saying, and I experienced a high like no other.

When I finished, all I heard was the applause from the Nuyorican crowd, and I knew at that moment that my old love of Hip Hop and my new love of the spoken word had been wed. I didn't go to the Café expecting to win a prize that night, but when I heard that I'd won second place I knew I had embarked on what seemed an impossible quest. I would maintain my day job while attending Hip Hop and spoken word events at night. I even broke out the turntables and started rocking at events again. "The Land Before the Rhyme" became my signature piece. It embodied every emotion I felt about what Hip Hop was and what it had become, and it bridged the gap between these two movements I so loved.

While some people did look at me with confused skepticism and criticism, others welcomed me like a breath of fresh air and immediately embraced me. I met activists and advocates, true believers and artists, people who cared as much about their communities as they did about themselves, and all of these connections helped me find meaning in my life. I walked among the poets who spoke out against injustice, corruption, sexism, racism, fascism, and materialism, and shed light on the plight of our communities. I began speaking about the culture of Hip Hop being raped. I was upset over the fact that the pioneers were being left destitute while major corporations continued to thrive off of something we helped build and create. Poetry gave me purpose.

In late 2005, my friend SueLye Guerra and I used my connections between the Hip Hop world and spoken word community to create the inaugural *Hip Hop Meets Spoken Wordz* fundraiser to benefit the homeless. With over 36 million Americans living below the poverty line and a staggering 28.2% of the Bronx population being afflicted, we decided to make this problem our platform. We brought together old-school legends Grandmaster Caz, Afrika Bambaataa, DJ Tony Tone, DJ Yoda, Whipper Whip, Grand Wizzard Theodore, L.A. Sunshine, JDL, Joe Conzo, and Pop-

Master Fabel with revolutionary artists Immortal Technique, Poison Pen, Diabolic, GI Joe, DPOne, Hasan Salaam, T-Weaponz, B-Boy Omega, Division X, El Grito de Poetas, Lemon, Shadokat, Props, DJ Laylo, La Bruja, Patty Dukes, and Rebel Diaz. These artists were true warriors in many community movements and to this day they continue to awaken the people to the real struggles we all face as a nation.

In the years that followed, Lizette and I would face an even greater challenge. After suffering a second miscarriage in 2002, Lizette began to seek treatment with the help of Dr. Gad Lavy, one of New England's top fertility doctors. We did manage to get pregnant during the in-vitro fertilization process only to suffer our third, and fourth miscarriages. I cannot begin to describe what this process has done not only physically, but also emotionally, to my wife. Being unable to conceive a child, what seems to be one of the most natural things for women to accomplish, will not stop us. To be reproductively challenged has brought an even wider sense of reality and drama to our already challenged lives. I know we will not stop our pursuit of being parents; Lizette will be a mother, and we will seek any avenue we need until our dream is realized.

At the same time, I would see my other baby Hip Hop grow right before my eyes as I continued to travel the country along with my young comrades as an elder statesman and mentor, bearing a message of love and hope. The power of Hip Hop is timeless and transcending.

I took on an aggressive calendar of events, which included TV, film and book projects, countless interviews, panels, speaking engagements, DJing events, and community fundraisers throughout the country. In July 2007 I traveled to Sydney, Australia, with Lizette. Standing at the top of Sydney's Blue Mountains humbled me completely. I stood there and looked out into the horizon as the tears rolled down my face, and gave thanks to the powers that be that I was alive to witness such beauty.

When we came home from our vacation I resigned from my job and a 25-year culinary career to pursue my dreams fulltime.

On November 3, 2006, I was billed to perform at the legendary Apollo Theater. As Lizette and I drove up, I saw my name *DJ DISCO WIZ* on the marquee in lights and it was then that I knew that anything was possible.

The Apollo Theater is considered the bastion of African-American culture and achievement, and one of the most fascinating chronicles in American history. It was constructed in 1914 on 125th Street in the heart of Harlem. Originally, it was named

Hurtig and Seamon's New Burlesque Theatre, and African-Americans were not allowed in the audience. In 1934, Ralph Cooper Sr. decided to do a live version of his already popular radio show, *Amateur Nite Hour at the Apollo*, at the Apollo Theater, then owned by the Schiffman family. Ella Fitzgerald was one of the first Amateur Night winners. In 1935, Bessie Smith made her Apollo debut followed by an unknown vocalist by the name of Billie Holiday. Soon thereafter, the Apollo became known as the place "where stars are born and legends are made," and has launched the careers of Stevie Wonder, Michael Jackson, and James Brown to name but a few of the icons that have crossed its stage. Tonight I would share in their historical legacy.

Backstage I greeted Kool Herc, Joe Conzo, Koe Rodriguez, and Ernie Paniccioli. I peeked out behind the curtain and saw a packed house. I couldn't believe that a Spanish kid from 183rd and Valentine Avenue was about to go on the stage of the world-famous Apollo Theatre. Lizette gave me a kiss and told me that she was very proud of me. As Ernie took his turn and walked out on stage, I looked back at my boys Koe and Joe and shot them both a smile. I knew I'd be getting called up at any moment and I was more nervous than I'd ever been in my entire life. I paced back and forth backstage thinking, "Damn, I hope I don't mess up my lines," and "Man, if I don't get on stage soon I'm really going to be sick."

I had survived a lifetime like no other to be standing right here, right now, at this moment and my throat began to close up in anticipation. When they finally announced me, I walked out on stage to the largest images of myself I'd ever seen on the JumboTron screen. With the bright lights shining down on me as the crowd went crazy, I truly understood that my life had really just begun.

I stepped to the podium and took a deep breath as I began to recite the very words that would define me…

> *Walk with me*
> *As I decipher these scriptures*
> *Struggles of my time*
> *The land before the rhyme*
>
> *Structured in the mind*
> *No need for the nine*
> *This complex life of mine*
> *1975 The movement has arrived*

Funny, of this no one can speak
A subject all too deep
A childhood that seems lost
Never had the means to floss
Abandoned by this cause

Often despised
Even criticized
How would I surmised
To this my only prize

No ends could be made
For the price we would pay
Economically strapped
No time for a nap

Cause this is about to go down

The boogie down was burning
My people yearning
Just to get a piece of the pie
My minds eye
Is as big as the sky

So who's to blame
For the circumstances aimed
At the unspoken names
Pawns to the game
This shit remains the same

The city with no fate
A place to escape
183rd, oh you never heard
Now that was the place to be

To see poetic street warriors

Turntable masters
Childhood dreams of mine
An art form divine
A land before the rhyme

We wired our system to a Lamppost
DJ battles for Years to boast
The stage was set
Here comes the test
The chosen ones to be so blessed

Two turntables above my chest
The mixer cued to do the rest
This would be the Weapon of choice
This music speaks it is our voice

The beauty of it all to be
This life we leave for you to see
For things that were just what they seemed
We knew of who we were to be
But lived for more than what we dreamed

For what you sow you reap
A junkie for a beat
In the parks I creep
The perfect scratch I seek
We ruled these fucking streets

A pioneer you say
From way back in the day
No royalties to pay
No riches came our way

No faking the funk
As the base would thump
The treble got me high

My revolution has arrived

Hip Hop supreme
No cheddar no bling
Guided by knowledge
No need for the cream

So tell me now
Can you answer this riddle?
Never have so few
Done so much for so little

We spit you out to chance
In a b-boy stance
Never to realize
What would be the prize

Who would have known
Industry now owned
Globally world known
Our baby is full grown

And although the legend goes
We birthed this flow
But who the fuck are we
Nobody knows

Call me the mixer
For the mixer is me
I rock the speakers
And the speaker is me

You seek the teacher
The teacher is me
I am Hip Hop
And Hip Hop is me…

Acknowledgments:

I would like to give thanks to everyone who has helped me along on my never-ending journey, and if I have forgotten to mention anyone please forgive me. - To my mother Anna Cira Cedeño (RIP), I miss you beyond words. For the love of my life Lizette Fonte-Cedeño, - Thank you for finding me and loving me beyond all measures, for daring me to live a life that I could have never imagine possible. For being all woman, ever sun, ever moon, everlasting, a complete partner in every sense of the word. Thank you for traveling endlessly through the shadows of time with me, breaking down all barriers and limitations with your grace, boundless desire for life and eternal love. To my beautiful daughter Tammy T. Cedeño, I love you. Thank you for giving me the chance to right all of the wrongs between us by blessing me with four incredible grandchildren - Cameron, Phoenix, Moses, and Savana. They give me purpose, will, and desire to dream beyond my imagination. To Mrs. Helen Jackson & family, I want to thank you for your leadership and strength, I am forever grateful to you. To Bayo and Mark Stevenson & family, thank you for the love & support. My father Alberto Nieves Cedeño (RIP), I forgive you. My stepfather Jenario Rodriguez (RIP), thank you for being a good husband to my mother, I miss you so much. My brother Ricardo Cedeño & family, I miss having you in my life. My grandmother Virginia Nieves (RIP), whenever I cook I think of you. To the Garcia family and all of my family member's aunts and uncles & cousins, thank you. My mother-in-law Gilda Fonte, thank you for stepping in and loving me when I abruptly lost my mother. I will always be your white rabbit. My brother-in-law Michael and his wife Annette Fonte, I love you both very much. Canderlario "Macho" Fonte (RIP), I miss you! I know you would have been very proud of me. To my grandmother-in-law Serafina Richardson "La Mulata de Fuego" may God give you many more years to celebrate life. To Patrice Yaglowski, Dr. Ellen Steele, Robert Augustyn, Eliza Orfao-Smernoff, Regina Krieger, Francine Cruz, Chris Mercado, Solvei Mckenna, Carrie Cusumano-Serhan, thank you for always being there for my wife Lizette. To all the doctors who saved mine and my wife's life against all odds, Dr. Robert Gelfand, Dr. Harry Gruenspan, Dr. Norris K Lee, Dr. Xu and Dr. Gad Lavy who gave me and my wife the greatest gift of all, thank you! To my childhood friends The East Side Boys- Karim "Mico" Neito, Anthony "Tony Rome" Neito (RIP), Solie Neito, Joey Adams (RIP), Patrick Adams, Gregory Joshua & Pierre, Robert "Chino" Rivera, Elvis "Papo" Negron, Tony Sunshine, Benny & Eddie, George, John "Skipper"

Jackson & Danny Jackson, John, Peter & Alex Cruz, Ali 3, Mouse, Husen, Michael "Sully" Sullivan I miss you all and often think of the good times, no matter where I go in this vast world I am forever a East Side Boy from 183rd. My little cousin Elvis "junior" Quiñones, you walk with me. To my first partner, childhood best friend and brother from another mother GrandMaster Caz & family, I love you bro, thank you for always being by my side, Hip Hop or not, our lives will forever be linked together. Ivan Sanchez & family how can I ever thank you? Only you and I know the tough and impossible road that we had to travel in order to make this book a reality. From the moment I read your first book – *Next Stop* I knew without a doubt that you were the only man up for the task, I love you like a brother, thank you for believing in me and following me around with your tape recorder, for crying with me and allowing me to release a lifetime of pain on you, I know that my nightmares will haunt you forever…Jenoyne Adams - Bliss, thank you for being the super agent pit-bull that you are! For your love and support and for never ever giving up on our book. To Sara Rosen, Daniel Power, Craig Cohen, Robert Avellan, Will Luckman, Kiki Bauer, Wes Del Val, Craig Mathis, Tami Mnoian, Viviana Morizet, Charles Requina, Orkan Benli, Jenny Jianai Chen & powerHouse Books, thank you for all the love and support and for believing in me, you have truly made my dreams come true. Suelye Guerra, thank you for inspiring me. Juan Sahah & family, thank you for teaching a little kid from the Bronx how to be a professional Chef. Orlando "BBoy Omega" Rodriguez, thank you for always believing in me, you are the man behind the man! No doubt! Carlito Rodriguez, thank you for bringing my legacy back to life bro, I am forever grateful. DJ Tony Tone, thank you for always being there, the gigs were endless and the memories timeless. Joe Conzo, thank you for the love and support. Charlie Ahearn & Jim Fricke it's been truly an honor to call you a friend. Jeff Chang, thank you for the valuable advice and building sessions, you are by far the humblest dude in the game. Jamel Shabazz, thank you for mentoring me, you are without a doubt my big brother. DJ Oxygen Crate digger supreme, thank you for the endless blessing's of Vinyl, but above all thank you for being a friend. James "Koe" Rodriguez & Christy Milanes, thank you for all of your creative input and vision. Marianne Williamson thank you for your spiritual guidance. To my first Hip Hop Crew the Mighty Force – DJ Casanova Fly, Prince Whipper Whip, Dota Rock, DJ Mighty Mike, Mr. T, Kool Kev & Pambaataa. Together we blazed a hell of a trail; I will never ever forget you. Saul Williams, thank you for inspiring me. Adam Bach - The Originators thank you for supporting me throughout the years. Ray Riccio & Ed

Riccio (RIP) - Sedgwick & Cedar, Oscar, Cas & Haps -Hard 8, Iman-Vintige clothing, Guerrilla Republik, Phat Farm, Luis A. Mateo - AZ God Empire, Tommy Lee-Amerikan Lyff, Pete-Ethnycity, Marc Ecko, Armory Chicago, Kareem Campbell-Lexani, Dean Stanton & Michael May - Rane, Stanton, Russell Brown - Ortofon, Ikey. Immortal Technique, you are the future. Bobbito Garcia, thank you for all the support bro. Lemon, Bom 5,Props, Marxman, High Priestess, MC Kess, Lah Tere, Rodstarz & GI-Rebel Diaz, Hasan Salaam & The 5th Column, Eli Efi, Gabriela Garcia Medina, Division X, Alvare, T-Weaponz, Rugged n Raw & KupiArts, Patty Dukes & Rephstar, Mo Browne, Jive Poetic, Red Clay, Ngoma, Rainmaker, Caitlin Meissner, Aja Monet, Barbara La Guerrera, Nightwalker, Diabolic, Sputnik Brown, Abundance Child, Mauikai Gold, Madd Illz, Am I Am, Poison Pen, Boca Floja, Precisescience, La Bruja, Mz Nancy, Iz The Truth, El Grito de Poetas, Shadokat, Survivor, DJ DPOne, DJ Gi Joe, DJ Laylo, DJ Sucio Smash, DJ Johnny Juice Rosado, DJ Tony Touch, DJ Camilo, DJ Eddie B Swift, DJ Rod 1, DJ Boo of the Juggaknots, DJ Chela, DJ Hapa, DJ Tito, Mangani, DJ Outlaw, DJ Nomadik, Claudia "DJ Soyo" Calleros, DJ Rockin Rob, DJ Vlad, DJ Rio Lopez, Dennis da Menace, DJ Chef, DJ Bestout, DJ Jazzy Jay, DJ AJ, Ivan "Doc" Rodriguez, DJ Lovebug Starski, DJ Ethos, J.D.L. Coldcrush Brothers & Money Ray (RIP), The Fantastic 5, The Treacherous 3, DJ Breakout & Baron, The L Brothers- Mean Gean & Grandwizzard Theodore, Afrika Bambaataa & The Mighty Zulu Nation thank you for enlightening me, Kool Herc thank you for creating a worldwide platform, DJ Clark Kent, Coke La Rock, Chuck Chillout & DJ Red Alert thank you for being a good friend, Awesome Two, DJ J-Rocc & The Beat Junkies, Mellow Man Ace, thank you hermano. Majesty, Mami Montana, Mare 139, James Top, Tracy 168, Dug1, Duro, Blade, LEE Quiñones, Judy Torres, K-7, Rabb Love, Trig-One, Grandmaster Melle Mel, Stay High 149, TAKI 183, PHASE 2, Kurtis Blow, Afrika Islam, Alien Ness, Bill Adler, Buddy Esquire, Busy Bee, Keith Cowboy (RIP), Disco King Mario (RIP), DJ Hollywood, Eddie Cheba, El Dorado Mike, Fab 5 Freddy, Nelson George, Frosty Freeze (RIP), Funky 4 + 1, DJ Jazzy Jeff, Grandmaster Flowers, Grand Master Flash, GrandMixer D.S.T, Henry Chalfant, Baby Huey (RIP), James Brown (RIP), James Bond, Rock Steady Crew, Jimmy Dee, Jo Jo, Ken Swift, Crazy Legs, Tools of War - Christie & Pop-Master Fabel Pabon, Mr. Freeze, Mr. Wiggles, Kevie Kev, K.K. Rockwell, The Bronx Boys, TBB, DJ Rob, Kid Creole, Kool Lady Blue, Martha Cooper, Pee Wee Dance, The Nigga Twins, Pete DJ Jones, Prince Paul, Phase II, Pistol Pete, Russell Simmons, LL Cool J, Run DMC, Jam Master Jay (RIP), Starchild La Rock, T La

Rock, Water Bed Kev, Black Dot. DJ Yoda & the Crash Crew, the Universal Federation of Hip Hop. The Dynamic Rockers, The Electric Boogaloos, The Gestapo Crew, The Mercedes Ladies, Trac 2, Public Enemy & Chuck D, Krs-One, D-Nice, A Alikes, Al Pizarro, Ariel Fernandez, Candice Clarke, Mecca aka Grimo, Alex Norman- PNC Entertainment. Andre Torres – Wax Poetics. Sole Junkie, Robert BBoyNYC , CT finest-Masters of Sound-DJ Love Kid & Terrible T, King Uprock, Charlie Uprock, Buzz 1, Big Mike, Big Banks, Special K, Daddy O, Dallas Pen, Dan the beat man, Dope Dave, Nene Ali, Nasiha Rose, David Yellen, Rosa Clemente, Rosette & Luis Reynolds, Rocafella, Rist.1 Top, Rich Medina, DJ Spinna, Raquel Z. Rivera, Melody 'Be, Dis,' Zai, Kid Rock, Patricia Lady P. Perez, Paradise, Paola Cancellieri, Oveous Maximus, Nicole Elieff, Jacqueline "Promise" Amuzie, Natalia Linares, Minister Server, Mikey 1 Soul, Mike Relm, Mighty Mike C, Frankie Needles & Mica Camacho – One Nation Mun2, Mark Riley, Lucky Strike, Lucio Dutch, Lorocka, Liza Garza, Lisa Kahane, Rodrigo Sanchez-Chavarra, Lea Chavez, Lance & Krista Morton, Lady Osofly Yarrow Lutz, Keith Claxton, K. Swift, Juice Jonze, Johan Kugelberg, G-UNet, Jesse Shysti Perez-Latin Rap Conference, J. Square, Philip Mlynar- Hip Hop Connection, Farrah Rios - Hip Hop Culture Center, Brian-Hip Hop Game, Hansel Balbuena, Rose Marie Mandes & family, Susanne Stemmler, Dr. Mark Naison & Dr. Oneka La Bennett – Fordham University, Dr. Mark Katz – University of North Carolina, Dr. Mark Anthony Neal – Duke University, Katherine A. Reagan, Ira Revels, Angela Herrera & Benjamin A. Ortiz – Cornell University, Alejandro Oscar Martinez, Timothy Jones, Nile Rodgers and Chic, Fred Buggs, Yerbabuena, My crew from - Urban Latino Radio.com, SimplyRadio, East Village Radio, Capital P - The Block, Hot 97, WBLS, SiTv, WBLI, Divine-Lavoe Revolt, Zee Santiago - The Trinity International Hip-Hop Festival, Brooklyn Hip Hop Festival, Brooklyn Bodega, Ben Herson-Nomadic Wax, The Temple of Hip-Hop, Byron Hurt, Melissa Noelle Green, Baba Israel, Tem Blessed, iLL-Literacy, Ernie Paniccioli, Yenexis "Yenny", Cindy Suga Rush, CX Kidtronix, Lauren Mace, DJ Wendy Goods, Ras, Supersize Spanishfly Lynx Garcia, Myk Jones, Ace "I'm in the mf books" Andretti, AC – Extravagangstara Radio, Anthony White (RIP), Steven Post (RIP), Brian Ward, The Crew from *Rock Docs NY77: The Coolest Year in Hell* - Henry Corra, Jonathan Mayo, Sara Sawyer, Jeremy Amar, Nanette Burstein, Brad Abramson & Warren Cohen- Vh1, OV 139, Frankie El Gato Figueroa & Team Gato, Fat Joe, Big Pun (RIP), Cuban Link & The Terror Squad, *The Source Magazine, Vibe, XXL*, AllHipHop.com, *Urban Latino Magazine*, The Bronx Museum of the Arts, La

Peña de Bronx, Picture the Homeless, The American Cancer Society, The Momentum Project, The Union League Club, Felix Gonzales & family, Vincent Gazzillo & family, The University Club, Graham Windham Harlem Day Care Center, to the student body at Mount St. Michael Academy, Cathedral High School, St. Barnabus High School & Stamford and Fairfield high schools, Thank you for supporting and giving my wife her best years as an educator. To all my brothers up north putting in time, stay strong *mi gente*, and remember that no matter what your current situation, it is never ever hopeless. *The Daily News*, *The New York Times*, *New York Post*, Diana & Barry Gould, Andrew Sullivan & Kerry wills - *Stamford Advocate*, *Village Voice*, *Hartford Advocate*, Unity Church of NYC, April Sims & The poet Man. Davey D, Donald D, Fatbeats, *Don Diva Magazine*, Capicu Poetry & Cultural Showcase, The Nuyorican Poets Café, Bowery Poetry Club, The World Famous Apollo Theatre, BrownPride.com, Burnside Avenue crew, Robert Pilichowski & the Crew from – All Out War, Bosco & Bella, thank you for bringing us so much happiness. Tara Brown & Joe No say, thank you. My people at GrandGoods, Myspace.com, Facebook.com, Xiomara Medina, April Lee Hernandez, Luis Antonio Ramos, Casper Martinez, Scout Tufankjian. To President Barack Obama, thank you for inspiring me and the country into believing in hope. To every person I ever hurt and to the unfortunate soul, whose life collided with me that fateful night in 1978, there is not a day that goes by that I don't think of you, please forgive me for I did not know what I was doing. To every person who ever helped me, for every venue I ever rocked, to every fan who ever reached out and supported me, thank you from the bottom of my heart, I am forever grateful to you all, you have inspired and touched my life like you could have never imagined…

— DJ Disco Wiz

First and foremost I want to thank God for giving me the talent to write the stories no one else seems to care enough to write.

Mi madre, Patricia for being the strongest women in my life. My beautiful little ladies, Heaven, Starr and Anesa Redd – everything I do when I wake up in the morning is so that you can be proud of me. Stormy and Christal for being wonderful mothers to my children.

To Bill, Krissy, Tanya & Jorge for lending me gas money for another trip to New York in search of the next great book.

To all my nieces and nephews: Meghan, Jordan, Alezia, Jesi, Nyko, Jayanna & Zoë…you are the future of this family.

To Luis "DJ Disco Wiz" Cedeño and Lizette Cedeño…for having the confidence in me and allowing me to help share this story with the world. Through the ups and downs we always knew the outcome would be special. I love you both!

To Sara Rosen for seeing what not many others saw. You are a true visionary and pioneer in regards to bringing this culture to life! Daniel Power—I've want to be a part of the powerHouse family ever since *Back in the Days*…thanks for the opportunity. To Craig Cohen for your tireless efforts and Robert Avellan for designing a fly book. Also to the entire powerHouse family…I'm glad I found a home with you all!

To Big Smooth for holding me down on "all" my trips to New York, you'll always be my brother.

To Yanira Valentin for answering the one question that seemed unanswerable.

My agent, Jenoyne Adams for sticking with the project and believing in it…my sister April Lee Hernandez & my brother Jose Castillo. My entire Two-Percenters Clique: La Bruja, Joe Conzo, Jamel Shabazz, Lynx Garcia, Ras & Myk Jones, Lady Picasso…if you know who the Two-Percenters are, you are most likely family…if not, only honesty and loyalty will bring you in.

To my entire family—the Torres family, the Ubinas family, Febos, Betancourts, the Redds, Damonds, DeSilvas, Barnes, Sabettis, Schwartzs, and on and on. I love you all the same!

Anyone and everyone who ever "helped" me along the way and never expected anything in return. You know who you are and I love you all the same…

All my boys in the hood—one day you'll find a way out…the truth is in the story!

All those who died in the struggle…you remain forever in my heart and soul…

—Ivan Sanchez

DJ Disco Wiz Mixtape

Pete Rock & CL Smooth – They Reminisce Over You – Elecktra
Nas – N.Y. State of Mind – Columbia
Wu Tang – Bring the Ruckus – Loud
Wu Tang – Wu-Tang: 7th Chamber – Loud
Eric B & Rakim – I know you Got Soul – 4th & B'way
Main Source feat. Akinyele, Joe Fatal, Nas – Live at The Barbeque – Wild Pitch
Original Flavor – Can I Get Open – Atlantic
Ultramagnetic MCs – Poppa Large (East Coast Remix)/
        (West Coast Remix) – Mercury
Chuck Chillout & Kool Chip – I'm Large –Polygram
Fu Schnickens – True FuSchnick – Jive
Eric B & Rakim – I Aint No Joke – 4th & B'way
K-Solo – Real Solo Please Stand – Atlantic
Ol Dirty Bastard – Brooklyn Zoo – Elektra
Ol Dirty Bastard – Shimmy Shimmy Ya – Elektra
Kool G Rap & DJ Polo – Poison – Cold Chillin
Flavor Unit feat. Freddy Foxx – Crazy Like a Fox (The Beef Is On) – Fat Beat
Cypress Hill – Hand on the Pump – Ruffhouse
Dr Dre feat. Snoop Dog – Deep Cover – Death Row
Big Pun feat. Fat Joe – Twinz (Deep Cover 98) – Loud
Public Enemy – Public Enemy # 1 – Columbia
Schoolly D – Am I Black Enough For You – Jive
Schoolly D – Saturday Night – Jive
KRS One – Step into a World – Jive
Baby Huey – Listen to Me – Curtom
John McLaughlin – Planetary Citizen – Columbia
James Brown – Give It Up or Turnit A Loose – King
Dennis Coffey and the Detroit Guitar Band – Son of Scorpio – Sussex
Roxanne feat. UTFO – Roxanne's Back Side – Select

MC Shan – The Bridge – Cold Chillin

Michael Viner's Incredible Bongo Band – Apache – Mr Bongo

Jimmy Castor Bunch – It's Just Begun – Salsoul Records

Yellow Sunshine – Yellow Sunshine – Gamble

Ultramagentic MC's – Funky – Next Plateau Entertainment

Herbie Hancock – Rockit – CBS

Eric B & Rakim – Don't Sweat the Technique – 4th & B'way

Eric B & Rakim – Eric B for President – 4th & B'way

Special Ed – Think About It – Profile

D-Nice – My Name Is D-Nice – Jive

Boogie Down Productions – I'm still # 1 – Jive

T La Rock & Jazzy Jay – It's Yours – Partytime

LL Cool J – Rock the Bells – Def Jam

Black Sheep – The Choice Is Yours – Mercury

LL Cool J – Mama Said Knock You Out – Def Jam

Rob Base – It Takes Two – Profile

Doug E. Fresh – The Show – Reality

Slick Rick – Lick the Balls – Def Jam

Slick Rick – Children's Story – Def Jam

Fearless Four – Fearless Freestyle – Elektra

Lovebug Starski – At the Fever – Fever Records

Fearless Four – Rockin It – Elektra

Cold Crush Brothers – Fresh, Wild, Fly and Bold – Tuff City

Planet Patrol – Play At Your Own Risk (Remix) – Tommy Boy

Immortal Technique produced by DJ Green Lantern – Parole (Evil Genius Mix)
    – The 3rd World

It s Just Begun
The Epic Journey of DJ Disco Wiz, Hip Hop s First Latino DJ

© 2009 powerHouse Cultural Entertainment, Inc.
Text © 2009 Luis Cedeño and Ivan Sanchez
Photos © 2009 Luis Cedeño, Corra Films, Andrew Sullivan, and Joe Conzo
The Product © 2004 Luis Cedeño
The Land Before the Rhyme © 2004 Luis Cedeño
All flyers appear courtesy Luis Cedeño

Miss Rosen Editions

Published in the United States by powerHouse Books,
a division of powerHouse Cultural Entertainment, Inc.
37 Main Street, Brooklyn, NY 11201-1021
telephone 212 604 9074, fax 212 366 5247
e-mail: itsjustbegun@powerHouseBooks.com
website: www.powerHouseBooks.com

First edition, 2009

Library of Congress Cataloging-in-Publication Data

DJ Disco Wiz, 1961-
  It's just begun : the epic journey of DJ Disco Wiz, hip hop's first latino DJ / by Ivan Sanchez and Luis "DJ Disco Wiz" Cedeño.
    p. cm.
  ISBN 978-1-57687-494-3 (hardcover)
1. DJ Disco Wiz, 1961- 2. Disc jockeys--New York (State)--New York--Biography. I. Sanchez, Ivan, 1972- II. Title.
  ML429.D54A3 2009
  782.421649092--dc22
  [B]

                          2008055083

Hardcover ISBN 978-1-57687-494-3

Printing and binding by Sun Fung Offset Binding Company, China

Book design by Robert Avellan

A complete catalog of powerHouse Books and Limited Editions is available upon request;
please call, write, or visit our website.

10 9 8 7 6 5 4 3 2 1

Printed and bound in China

DATE			